PRACTITIONER RESEARCH

PRACTITIONER RESEARCH

The reflexive social worker

Roger Fuller and Alison Petch

OPEN UNIVERSITY PRESS
Buckingham • Philadelphia

Open University Press
Celtic Court
22 Ballmoor
Buckingham
MK18 1XW

email: enquiries@openup.co.uk
world wide web: http://www.openup.co.uk

and
325 Chestnut Street
Philadelphia, PA 19106, USA

First Published 1995
Reprinted 1999

A catalogue record of this book is available from the British Library

ISBN   0 335 19323 4 (hb)   0 335 19322 6 (pb)

Library of Congress Cataloging-in-Publication Data
Fuller, Roger, 1944–
    Practitioner research : the reflexive social worker / Roger Fuller
and Alison Petch.
      p.   cm.
    Includes bibliographical references (p.   ) and index.
    ISBN 0–335–19323–4 (hard).—ISBN 0–335–19322–6 (pbk.)
    1. Social service—Research—Methodology.   2. Social service—
Research—Methodology—Case studies.   I. Petch, Alison, 1950–
II. Title.
HV11.F854   1995
361.3'2'072—dc20   95–8638
                                                                     CIP

Typeset by Graphicraft Typesetters Ltd, Hong Kong
Printed in Great Britain by Biddles Ltd, Guildford and King's Lynn

Contents

Preface

This book is based on ideas developed in the Practitioner Research Programme run by staff of the Social Work Research Centre at the University of Stirling since 1991. The idea of running a programme for inexperienced researchers drawn from social work (and related) practice was in part a response to demand, as described in Chapter 2. At the start, we had no idea whether the enterprise would work, and we are particularly indebted to the first group to come on the programme (some of whose work is represented in Part Three of the book) for demonstrating that it could. What is more, they and their successors have claimed to enjoy it, and, perhaps a little to our surprise, so do we.

All those involved in the development of the programme were deeply saddened by the sudden death of Carole Addison during the initial planning for its first delivery. Carole was to have acted as consultant to the programme. She had already proposed as a modification to the original outline the addition of the call-back day at the half-way stage, a feature which is now believed to be one of the keys to the success of the programme.

Our belief in the programme's effectiveness in enabling successive groups of practitioners without research experience to carry out small-scale studies in their own agencies has been widely endorsed, and the book sets out the principles of practitioner research as they have evolved during the four years of the programme's life to date. The general approach is practical and demystificatory; we have tried to see the problems of designing and carrying out research through the eyes of the practitioner.

Our experience of working with practitioners strongly suggests that people learn about research heuristically – that is to say, by doing it; appropriate guidance is provided with the aid of practical examples and exercises, and with judicious help at the level of general research concepts and principles, but without labouring technical or theoretical issues. The book reflects this emphasis on striking a balance between the practical and the intellectually adequate. We focus on the tools of the trade, and on solving problems as they arise. We are realistic about the opportunities available to practitioners for getting access to specialist libraries or to sources of technical help, and we are particularly concerned to offer the kind of support which will enable them to complete a study once they have embarked on it. Ideal ways of proceeding which feature in some textbooks can sometimes be the enemy of the feasible.

The book is in four parts. In Part One, we set out the rationale, dimensions and context of research conducted by social work practitioners, discuss some of the problems that need to be addressed by those seeking to promote practitioner research, and describe our approach to resolving them. Part Two details what is involved, and what the novice researcher needs to be aware of, in setting up a study, choosing appropriate methods, carrying it out, and reporting on it, and is illustrated by real-life examples from programme participants. In Part Three we present some examples of studies carried out and written up by practitioners themselves, so that readers may see a range of what is possible (the references for the studies, unlike the rest of the book, follow at the end of each chapter). Finally, Part Four includes an afterword, discussing some issues of the impact, significance and future of practitioner research.

We must make many acknowledgements. We would like to place on record our appreciation of the inspirational help and advice of the late Carole Addison, a pioneer in the field, when we were planning the programme. We thank all the practitioners who have taken part in the programme, a full list of whom appears in Appendix 1; it is through their collaborative efforts that we have worked up the material that the book presents. We are grateful both for the initial support of the Joseph Rowntree Foundation and the personal interest of its director of research Janet Lewis, which enabled the programme to get off the ground. The otherwise unsung efforts of our colleagues at the Social Work Research Centre have been vital to keeping it in the air. June Watson has been a cheerfully competent organizer of the residential courses that feature in the programme, and has coped nobly in the production of the manuscript with its wayward authors.

Part One

Practitioner research:
the idea and the reality

Chapter 1

Why practitioner research?

Research conducted by practitioners is an idea whose time has come. It is also full of hazards for the unprepared. In this book we set out some reasons why practitioners should venture into research, what skills they bring to bear upon it and what they need to learn, what perspectives they can provide which might enrich existing work, how they can set about it, what kinds of support and guidance they need to undertake it.

To the uninitiated, research can seem daunting. It variously conjures up images of white-coated boffins, dry-as-dust statisticians, deep thinkers, closely-typed and table-packed reports, the mystique of the expert. In some respects these stereotypes may be flattering to researchers, but research has other, less pleasing connotations: of ineffectuality and remoteness from the real world, of the exploitation of respondents, of political naivety. In addressing ourselves to practitioners in social work and similar fields, we wish to qualify some of this imagery. Our argument is that research, though not simple or capable of being carried out without technical knowledge, is not as mysterious as all that, and that it is possible for practitioners, with appropriate support and guidance, to enhance significantly their understanding of the tasks that they and their colleagues take on in their daily practice. We further suggest that it is possible to attain a productive marriage between the systematic intellectual enquiry which characterizes research and the tough-minded realities of life in social care agencies – indeed, that they are not necessarily opposed. And through such a marriage, we believe, a flow of practitioner research has much to contribute to the developing body of research on social work practice which to date has been largely conducted from outside.

We speak here, and throughout the book, of 'social work' or 'social care' since this is our domain, but our message is equally addressed to practitioners of other disciplines. In particular, given current developments in social policy, health and social care are frequently bracketed together because their boundaries are unclear and their practitioners work closely with each other, often on common problems. Concepts and practices treated here are equally applicable to many in the caring professions other than social workers, including occupational therapists, nurses, and community health workers, and indeed others across the spectrum of service delivery.

Some definitions and distinctions

In the field of social care, research comes in a variety of forms and is often divided into seemingly distinctive categories. These include: 'academic' and applied research, often and misleadingly thought to be at opposite poles; surveys, case studies, evaluations; experimental and hypothesis-testing studies; 'action research'; participative or collaborative research. The research field is especially prone to attaching different labels to approaches or concepts which, when peeled off, turn out to reveal phenomena which are not so different after all – something that is especially so when the terminology of different disciplines is compared. In particular, the concept of 'evaluation' with its associated notion of 'outcomes' has entered the culture of the public sector in the 1980s and 1990s and has generated an array of technical terms in different schools of thought and different disciplines: process and goal evaluation, formative and summative evaluation, inputs and outputs, intermediate and final outcomes, service-based and client-centred outcomes, and so on (Goldberg and Connolly, 1981; Lishman, 1984; Knapp, 1984; Cheetham *et al.*, 1992).

Although some of the terms above may appear rather different from each other, the differences are often more apparent than real. They all, for example, require the application of a common core of research skills: in formulating research questions or hypotheses, in collecting or utilizing data and analysing it in ways which address the questions, in interpreting the findings, and in communicating the results in writing or orally. They all seek as the objective an improved understanding of the phenomena under study – whether such understanding is to be put to immediate use in practice by practitioners themselves, has longer-term implications for management or policy, or influences the way we think conceptually or theoretically, or (frequently) some combination of all of these.

Furthermore, the categories above contain much that overlaps. For example, 'academic' research in social care may come dressed in rather more abstract or theoretical clothes than studies undertaken outside academic bodies, but will almost certainly be 'applied' in the sense that its findings have some purchase on the decisions of policymakers and practitioners. Evaluation may take place through surveys, case studies, experimental studies, or action research. When we speak of 'practitioner research' we mean simply research undertaken by practitioners; we intend no implication in principle that particular research approaches, strategies or methods will be used by practitioner–researchers, or that a particular style of research characterizes their efforts. It may be that in practice, however, constraints of time and limited access to expertise mean that practitioners are well advised to stick with the tried, tested and simpler methods, and that the social care subject matter may make certain approaches more appropriate than others (see Chapter 4).

A particular mention is needed about action research as a category, since it is a term often used loosely to refer to any research conducted in real-life situations and since in other fields such as education it appears to be virtually synonymous with research undertaken by practitioners. Action research is a complex topic with competing interpretations of its meaning and application (Rapoport, 1970; Kemmis and McTaggart, 1981; Elliott, 1991). For some, it is defined by a focus on studies of episodes, often of the case-study type, in 'real' agencies; for others by the relationship between the researcher and the subject; for yet others by practitioners being themselves the researcher. As we understand the term, action research denotes a style of research involvement which builds in a 'special relationship' between the researcher and the researched, whereby study proceeds in jointly planned phases, each one culminating in the feeding back of results from the researcher to practitioners, who then modify practice accordingly and plan the next phase of research to monitor the effects of the changes.

Action research or practitioner research, especially in the education field, has drawn particular impetus from the work of Schön (1983), who entitled his book *The Reflective Practitioner*. For Schön, the reflective practitioner is one whose practice is accompanied by 'thinking in action', a concept he uses to distinguish the style of thinking deployed by experienced practitioners from that of, say, the academic commentator who takes abstract or theoretical concepts and then applies them to particular situations. Although this account of how professionals think has been qualified or contested by subsequent commentators (Brown and McIntyre, 1993), we are influenced by this vision of an intimate and interactive relationship between thinking and action, as shown by the modified use we have made of it in our own subtitle. The change to 'reflexive' seems to capture more accurately the self-referring nature of the concept.

The action–research paradigm, however, with its seductive view of the relationship between research and action, has been found difficult to bring off in practice. When the researcher is a non-practitioner, it is easier said than done to maintain the phasing of the research and action elements of the partnership. When the researcher is the practitioner, there is a requirement for a long-term commitment on the part of agency managers to sustain the endeavour and take on board the findings. Although the practitioner–researcher may be well placed to attempt an action–research approach, we do not see it as by any means the natural or necessarily the recommended course to follow.

The practitioner–researcher will, however, be more likely to be working in a participative or collaborative style. This approach to research, initially developed to reproduce some of the features of action research without its more problematic feedback loop, involves collaboration with others more traditionally thought of rather demeaningly as the 'subjects' of research in the development of ideas about what to study; it may also include their active participation in carrying out the study and in interpreting results. Thus initial thoughts about researchable topics and priorities may have been developed collectively in formal or informal discussions with professional colleagues or with groups of users or carers. The latter may then be involved in collecting and analysing data, or (perhaps more often) in discussions about the interpretations of findings and their dissemination. In this way, both the choice of topic and the processes of research are democratized, the research has wider ownership than the researcher alone, and there is an extra level of commitment both to its successful completion and to acting on the findings.

Practitioner research, then, does not entail any particular method or strategy of research, and is not in itself a special category of research. The whole spectrum of research designs and skills is available to the researcher, constrained only by any practical limitations in the agency setting or in the researcher's own knowledge or access to expert advice. The practitioner–researcher is, however, well placed to develop a participative style of research engagement with both colleagues and the users of services, in some respects better so than the externally based researcher, and to capitalize on the advantages offered.

Why should practitioner research be encouraged?

Social work needs research for many reasons, both internal and external to the social work profession (Cheetham *et al.*, 1992). These include the need to establish a research base for a profession subject to much ill-informed criticism, the demands of politicians for value for money, and the ethical obligations for practice to be aware of empirical evidence for its effectiveness. But why should practitioners themselves do it? Why not leave it to the so-called experts?

Research has achieved a growing profile in social work in recent years. Its impact has been felt in a variety of ways. Successive legislation (the Children Act 1989 and the introduction of Community Care) has been significantly influenced by research findings. There has been a proliferation within social work of research-flavoured concepts like performance indicators, quality assurance and evaluation. Justified demands for professional accountability, prompted by both external criticisms and a growing realization that research has produced positive findings for social work effectiveness (Macdonald and Sheldon, 1992), have been accompanied by the endorsement by both the British Association of Social Workers and the Central Council for the Education and Training of Social Workers (CCETSW, 1989 and its successors) of research as an important element in the professional repertoire of social workers.

At the very least, then, and perhaps in a somewhat defensive spirit, there is a case for social workers needing to develop a degree of research-mindedness as a means of understanding some of the pressures brought to bear upon social work, of critically responding to the demands made upon them by legislation and by the general movement towards greater accountability, especially in some of its cruder manifestations. 'Research-mindedness' has a number of components, including an awareness of the scope and limitations of research, an ability to read critically the claims which emerge from research studies or from policy changes which purport to be based upon them and a sympathetic attitude towards research which may be conducted in a practitioner's own worksetting. There may be various ways in which this may be achieved, but one of the most effective is for practitioners to have the experience of grappling with the problems of carrying out a piece of research for themselves.

More positively, Everitt *et al.* (1992) see the development of research awareness as a means of 'reclaiming professionalism', of asserting the value, and values, of the professional discipline of social work over and against those features of its bureaucratic and ideological setting which limit its liberating potential: 'welfare professionalism needs to be reclaimed from managerialism and from the "bourgeois improvers"'(p. 3). From this perspective, the practitioner who has acquired research skills and the critical antennae which develop alongside them will be a more complete professional: better able to challenge organizational or political constraints, more aware of the social structures which underlie the kinds of difficulties experienced by clients, more sceptical of taken-for-granted features of the world of social work. Practitioners will also develop a research appreciation capacity, being able to read research both more receptively and more critically, and to make use of it in thinking about implications for their own practice and about agency policies (Black, 1993). If practitioners are to be encouraged to take research into account in pondering issues of practice or management, they must be able to distinguish the rigorous from the weak and the relevant from the irrelevant in research accounts that come their way or that they seek out.

These considerations apply in the general approach to the task, but closer to the ground the research-minded practitioner knows better than most what questions could be addressed to increase understanding of the circumstances and problems of actual or potential service users and to improve service effectiveness. And at the level of practice, research skills can make more systematic and informed such basic social work tasks as gathering and collating information about individual clients, assessing resources and their likely efficacy, monitoring progress and evaluating effectiveness, and feeding information to service planners and policymakers.

More pragmatically, there is the consideration that such is the pressure on social workers to demonstrate their effectiveness at the tasks allotted to them by a sometimes dubious political process, that if they themselves do not involve themselves in carrying out the required research, it will be done by others who may be less sympathetic to the nature of those tasks. There are questions here of the social status of the social work profession, whose relatively low standing in the eyes of key constituencies as compared, say, with the medical professions, is probably due at least in part to its failure thus far to develop a social work equivalent to the tradition of clinical research.

Why social workers should do research	• to enhance basic professional skills • to produce more informed ways of being accountable • to increase the standing of the profession • to ensure a research base that is sympathetic to social work values

The development of research-mindedness among the providers of services has recently been endorsed in the Department of Health's research strategy for the personal social services (Department of Health, 1994), which sets its sights on promoting a more informed and research-based practice. The paper argues for the users of research, including practitioners as well as senior managers, to become more involved in setting research agendas, more appreciative of research issues, and generally more research literate; practitioner research, and the Practitioner Research Programme conducted at the University of Stirling, are specifically commended as a means of developing a sense of ownership among practitioners, described as 'fundamental to the development of a research culture' (p. 19).

Research and social work practice: complementary or different perspectives?

The social worker who accepts the arguments for becoming a practitioner–researcher and wishes to acquire research skills brings considerable advantages to the task, with perhaps a few disadvantages. The advantages stem in part from practitioners' own professional background, and in part from their insider position. To rehearse these briefly serves to highlight the areas on which would-be practitioner–researchers need to focus, and which are further developed in subsequent chapters of this book.

Thoughtful social workers start with a range of skills and experience which not only translate readily into a research framework but which may actually confer certain advantages over the traditional external researcher. First, their day-to-day experience gives them an unequalled degree of insight into, and knowledge of, the real problems which face both clients and service providers. Although they usually need help in distinguishing the researchable from the non-researchable, and the formulation of specific research questions is a considerable art, this knowledge and insight creates both the capacity to pinpoint the key general questions which research can most profitably address, and to understand the context of such questions in larger agency or community issues. In these respects practitioners enjoy advantages over external researchers, who are inevitably at a remove from the front line and commonly need intensive discussions with practitioners to confirm or refine definitions of what is important or what makes most sense.

Potentially at least, however, there is a corresponding disadvantage to this, in that practitioners may through habit-blindness have difficulty in seeing the wood from the trees. To adopt a research perspective one needs to stand back, to see a wider picture than is necessarily visible from the individual practitioner's workload. Similarly, it involves a certain distancing from the taken-for-granted conceptual and linguistic apparatus of the practitioner. Social work discourse (like that of other professions) is littered with jargon, with terms like 'prevention', 'needs', 'community' or 'support', which social workers will use as a kind of shorthand, thinking they know what they mean but sometimes having difficulty in describing them in the kind of operational terms required by research.

A second advantage is the clarity of thinking and analysis about problems and ways of tackling them that skilled social work requires, and for which they are not always given due credit. Social workers are familiar with the need to make judgements and distinctions about the problems faced by their clients and themselves. This includes distinguishing, where appropriate, between 'presenting' and underlying problems; between those aspects of a client's situation which can realistically be addressed through social work means and available resources, those which should be referred elsewhere, and those which are not amenable to effective intervention; and between those which are capable of short-term and longer-term resolution. They are also familiar with shuttling backwards and forwards between these different levels, so that the whole picture is kept in mind while a particular aspect of a client's situation is the focus.

Especially if a version of task-centred work is practised, social workers are skilled at identifying particular tasks and timescales and negotiating these with clients. Such habits of thought translate admirably into the researcher's need to analyse the way research problems are formulated, to disaggregate them and make an assessment about what is feasible and realistic to study with finite resources and time.

A third advantage which needs little elaboration is the fact that social workers are already (or should be) expert interviewers and recorders of data. There are some differences between the approach to be taken in research and social work interviews – the purposes of the two will not be identical – but they can be exaggerated. There is the same need to develop rapport, and the same issues of sticking to an agenda and of discriminating between relevant information and 'noise' arise. Similarly, social workers are familiar with the need to make an economical and usable record of the information and insight they assemble in daily practice and this again has its research equivalent in interview records or observation or field notes.

More mundanely, practitioners have knowledge of sources of data within their agency and, normally, ready access to them. Here again the insider has particular advantages, since external researchers are likely to be quite unsure what information is held where, and may have to go through lengthy negotiations in order to see it. Practitioners will not only be knowledgeable about the availability and location of data but also about the quality of records – what information is recorded systematically and reliably, what is inconsistently or vaguely noted.

There are, however, some adjustments in perspective which practitioner–researchers need quite consciously to make. Firstly, research has a different agenda and focus from that of practice, and different timescales. Most particularly, perhaps, it is not concerned with helping people, or at least not directly so, nor with solving organizational problems as they occur. Pay-offs of these kinds are usually longer-term matters, and practitioners who don a research hat must occasionally remember that they have temporarily thereby discarded that of the practitioner. Occasionally, too, they will find that in the interests of completing the research, practices which ordinarily would be changed may need to be held constant for the duration of the study.

Advantages of the practitioner perspective in research	• a research agenda rooted in knowledge of practice • complementary problem analysis and disaggregation skills • interviewing and recording skills • access to data

Disadvantages of the practitioner perspective in research	• closeness to social work pactice and terminology • unaccustomed to formulating research questions • a different focus • different kinds of sensitivity

Secondly, although practitioners are accustomed to working in a sensitive context, the kinds of sensitive or anxiety-creating issues which arise in research more commonly concern the practitioner's colleagues than clients or their families. Research scrutiny of professional practice may reveal examples of activities which are normally hidden, which may differ from managerial expectations, even some which the researcher frankly considers unprofessional. There are ethical issues here, which apply to all research but which are especially pointed in the case of the practitioner–researcher. What is the proper balance between obligations to service users, obligations to colleagues and the honouring of assurances of anonymity, and loyalty to an organization? It is preferable for the researcher to have considered these issues in advance, and (though this perhaps is a counsel of perfection) to have agreed in advance with participants a set of guidelines for dealing with them.

Willing the means

The previous section has not referred to what may seem the most serious set of obstacles in the way of the practitioner–researcher: the need to effect a significant transfer of what is assumed to be specialized and 'technical' knowledge to the inexperienced about the process of doing research. To the outsider, the technical apparatus of research often seems intimidatingly arcane and mysterious, and perhaps the *apparent* scale of the problem accounts for the relatively poorly developed state of practitioner research in social work. By what means can the desirable aim of arming the practitioner with research tools be achieved?

In fact, our experience would suggest that other factors are at least as important as the technical mysteries, and that probably the most important of these is time. Clearly it is difficult, if not impossible, to undertake a piece of research on top of the practitioner's normal work commitments. (In a profession like teaching, which is arguably under as much pressure as social work and which yet has a more developed tradition of practitioner research, at least there are long holidays!) Research demands time, and 'quality time' at that; it is not something that can be fitted in around other tasks in a spare half-hour here and there. Whether practitioners are undertaking a research-based dissertation in pursuit of an advanced part-time qualification, or attending a special programme like the Practitioner Research Programme at the University of Stirling, or simply and bravely doing a research study completely independently, they will need to have negotiated with managers and colleagues sufficient time to carry out the study. The problem arises, of course, of how much time is necessary, and the answer to this is likely to be at best arbitrary. What is particularly difficult for first-time researchers is that they may well be negotiating before they have started any course or acquired sufficient knowledge of the kind of time constraints implied by choices of method. Their estimates may well not be realistic, and in particular may underestimate the time required for analysis and writing up.

A vital requirement for guidance to practitioners, then, and probably a *sine qua non*, is the double message of realistic advice about the time implications of undertaking different kinds of research, and a firm commitment from managers that the time will be protected – often easier said than done in contemporary social work.

A second requirement, again at least as important in our own experience as the 'technical' factors, is moral support. Research is a lonely business, and a study will frequently not go according to plan – a combination which, especially for the unconfident, can lead all too easily to disillusion and drop-out. Programmes for practitioner–researchers, therefore, need to build in a system of moral as well as technical support. This can be achieved at a somewhat minimal level through the standard relationship with a supervisor, consultant, or advisor, but is greatly enhanced if the practitioner has access to a group of fellow researchers sharing similar problems.

Turning to the more technical realm, we have found that the priorities amongst the wide range of potential knowledge that practitioner–researchers need to acquire are:

- how to formulate specific researchable questions
- the appropriateness for different tasks and the logistics of different methods of collecting data
- techniques and logistics of different approaches to analysis
- the importance and variety of methods for disseminating findings.

The pitfalls are implicit in all this: starting off on the wrong foot with inadequately formulated research questions; unrealistic timetables; failure to appreciate the requirements of design and methodological choices; loss of nerve when things go wrong. All of these can lead to failure.

These, then, are the problems which managers who wish to encourage practitioner research, practitioners who undertake it, and academics who try to facilitate it need to be aware of and develop some means of solving. Apart from dissertations in initial qualifying training, most research undertaken by social work practitioners is in the context of a course leading to a higher qualification, whether a Master's degree in social research or through one of the few post-qualifying or advanced professional courses which feature research. In the former case, social care practitioners will be alongside students from other backgrounds, and teaching is unlikely to be geared to their particular professional context or interests; syllabi tend to include a range of material which, while fulfilling academic requirements for a general research education, will be of debatable relevance to practitioner research. Within professional social work, progress towards the creation of a strong research tradition seems likely to be slow. For a variety of reasons social work has been behind other disciplines in developing its potential for post-qualifying work, partly because of its starting point as a profession with a considerable number of non-graduates, partly because of employers' lack of interest in, and resources for, supporting post-qualifying training opportunities. In some ways the situation is less promising than in the past: the long-defunct journal *Case Conference* used regularly to publish research-based practitioner accounts of self-evaluated practice, case studies of individual clients, and the like, for which there is no current outlet in the UK, and little encouragement.

As suggested earlier, there is a considerable tradition of action research in education, with its own journal and an international network composed of teachers and academics interested in action research. This tradition, which has a number of competing theoretical allegiances, can give the impression that research by educational practitioners is flourishing. This appears on closer examination to be something of an exaggeration. Like social workers, teachers undertake higher-degree courses which require a dissertation by research, but there is less evidence of them carrying out research as part of their normal daily work. Practitioner research in education is conventionally classroom-based (for which there is no direct equivalent in social work) and predominantly qualitative or 'illuminative'.

Despite this perhaps pessimistic account, a number of texts have been published which seem to indicate burgeoning interest in practitioner research. The elementary handbook of Addison (1988) was succeeded by Whitaker and Archer (1989) who based their extremely useful methodological text on their experiences of working with a group of practitioner–researchers at the University of York (see Chapter 2), which has subsequently developed into a more structured partnership arrangement with a social services department. Broad and Fletcher's (1993) collection of practitioner-research studies was drawn from a higher-degree course at the then Cranfield Institute of Technology (though many of the participants were some way above basic-grade practitioner level). Books have begun to appear with titles like *Real World Research* (Robson, 1993) and

The Hard-Pressed Researcher (Edwards and Talbot, 1994) which are aimed mainly or in part at practitioner–researchers, though less in social care than in other fields.

Opportunities and hazards

To sum up, the promise of practitioner research is that it can contribute to the growing body of social work research in a distinctive manner, producing a small but significant flow of studies which are targeted on the concerns of practitioners and managers. It can also enhance the collective resources of social workers by stimulating research awareness, leading potentially to a more 'reflexive' profession, capable of learning from experience in more than anecdotal ways, to a better service for clients, and to an enriched view of the social worker's professionalism.

But the profession, and those concerned with its management and training, must will the means. Research by practitioners is not insurmountably difficult but it is not a straightforward add-on for a professional group already struggling with a permanently expanding workload. The hazards of failing to take account of the necessary ingredients are that the whole enterprise will fail to get off the ground, and practitioner research in social work fall into disrepute. Chapter 2 describes one approach to tackling the problems.

From idea to reality: a programme for practitioner research

This chapter will shift the focus from the general to the specific, outlining the challenges that had to be met in order to establish a successful practitioner-research programme. No apology is offered for the, at times, somewhat prosaic nature of certain of the dimensions that are explored; attention to such detail is, it is argued, a prerequisite for a successful outcome.

Evolution

The seeds for Stirling's practitioner-research programme were sown at a major conference on evaluating social work effectiveness organized by the Social Work Research Centre (SWRC) in 1987. As the conference closed, a practitioner remarked that, interesting though the major presentations had been, they had not really addressed the issues that had to be tackled by those who wished to pursue the evaluative route in their own workplace.

This comment hung in the air. Gradually the conviction grew that proactive steps should be taken to meet this expressed need. The first response was a bid for funding under a research training initiative mounted by the Economic and Social Research Council. Not surprisingly, perhaps, given the charting of somewhat unfamiliar waters, this application was not successful. More fruitful, however, was a subsequent bid to the Joseph Rowntree Foundation (or Memorial Trust as it was at this time).

Funding provided by the Trust over a three-year period for a bursary scheme for practitioners administered through the universities of Birmingham and Sheffield had recently come to an end. Under this scheme, bursaries had been awarded to eight social workers who had pursued a variety of projects, ranging from the implications of a new housing development for the work of a social services patch team to the needs of carers of people with AIDS and individuals' access to information about their rights under the Mental Health Act 1983. A particular emphasis had been laid on the dissemination of the findings from projects, although not necessarily through the standard publication routes.

The model for the Rowntree bursary programme was a highly individualistic one. Each bursary holder was linked to a supervisor, with the relationship developing very much according to individual needs. Those responsible for the scheme commented at the time

> Our approach to the scheme up to now has been a very individualistic one. This was intentional as we wanted to provide a very flexible way of enabling people to pursue their particular interests in ways that were appropriate to their circumstances. This has resulted in some very different projects, and in different sorts of outputs. However, we do feel that it would be useful to explore some more collective approaches to this scheme.

This more collective approach was exemplified by the development of a course offered on a day-release basis by York University in 1982, 1984 and 1986, 'Understanding Social Work Practice Through Designing and Conducting Research'. The experience of this initiative very much informs the discussion presented in Whitaker and Archer (1989). Eight practitioners each year pursued a piece of practice-based research under the guidance of the university. Despite, however, participants being motivated by having developed a 'burning interest' in their work situation, not a large number of these studies led to any final outcome. Subsequently the university has developed a closer, partnership model whereby individuals study part-time over a two year period on an MA course, 'Practice-related Research in the Helping Professions'.

The SWRC bid to Rowntree in 1989, originally entitled 'Evaluation on the Doorstep: A Programme to Help Social Workers Evaluate Activities Within their own Agencies', was developed in close collaboration with the late Carole Addison, then Principal Social Worker (Practice Research and Development) with Wandsworth Borough Council. She had been the author of a NISW workbook on the planning and negotiating of projects, then recently published as part of the Practice and Development Exchange (Addison, 1988). She had also had considerable experience of delivering practice evaluation courses in various forms and was very aware of the limitations placed by practice on practitioner research (1988: 5).

> All the available evidence suggests that only a minority of practitioners who begin investigative projects actually complete them. Fewer still go on to publish their results . . . You need to ask yourself

what your pay-off will be, and whether it will compensate for all the hard work that lies ahead.

Her workbook (given to all participants on the Stirling course) was designed to demystify the research process and to offer a pathway through the various stages. Our course proposal built on this base to offer staged input and a support mechanism.

The SWRC proposal acknowledged the contemporary concern with evaluative activity, but highlighted the obstacles that could impede the smaller scale, in-house initiative.

Experience shows that the extent to which individual social workers can carry out supervised evaluation depends in part on the impetus, advice and support available within social work agencies or on the regular help available from a research centre or similar body. Providing this help on an individual one to one basis is not particularly efficient, not least because it limits the opportunities social workers have to learn from and support each other in the evaluation of their activities.

Although the centrality of such activities was undisputed, it was recognized that local authorities and other agencies often found it difficult to allocate their limited resources to training in this area. This was a particular issue at a period when training budgets were already overcommitted to preparing staff for the implementation of the policies outlined in Caring for People. It was therefore considered important to access funding which would enable the training programme to be provided, at least in the first instance, free of charge.

The SWRC proposal differed from earlier models in focusing more narrowly on the evaluation of social work effectiveness, a strategy in line with the brief for the Centre activities as a whole. It was also perhaps more modest in intent in terms of the demands made on participants' time and agency resources. Preliminary enquiries to training officers in several agencies had identified support in principle for the programme, although little, as prefaced above, by way of resource allocation.

The Trustees of the Joseph Rowntree Foundation considered that the proposal 'would be a useful experiment'; funding in the order of £14 000 was allocated to run two complete cycles of the programme. These were mounted from January to September 1991 and January to September 1992, with intakes of 22 and 20, respectively. The format of the programme is presented in more detail below. In broad outline, however, an initial study period of three days based at the university is followed by a further two-day input nine months later. The group also meet for a day mid-way through the programme. During the intervening period, each individual has contact with a named member of the Centre staff for ongoing support and guidance.

Two further runs of the programme have now been completed, September 1993 to June 1994 and September 1994 to June 1995. Approximately one-quarter of the places each year are allocated to individuals working in the voluntary sector; the remaining participants have been from the nine mainland authorities in Scotland with a concentration in the central belt.

The outline for the SWRC programme attempted to draw from the experience of the earlier models, and in particular to address the issue of non-completion of projects. Both the Rowntree bursary programme and the York scheme had found that, despite initial enthusiasm and good intent, rather few studies had yielded some form of final output. The remainder of this chapter will explore the particular dilemmas of practitioner research and the practical steps which were taken in the development of the programme to address these challenges.

It is appropriate to distinguish at this point between, on the one hand, continuing monitoring and evaluation embedded within daily practice and, on the other, the specification of a time-limited evaluative project examining a specific aspect of practice. It is the latter endeavour which is the subject of the current programme, although in practice many of the techniques employed (Chapter 4) can be adopted to the more continuous process. As detailed above, a central aim of the programme was to extend research-mindedness within the practice setting. The aspiration was that evaluative activity should be seen as a potential within every workplace rather than the prerogative of the external agency or of specialists. To this end, the hope was that individuals selected for the programme would share their experience of becoming involved in research activity with others in their agency, rather than retaining it as an individual learning experience.

Challenges

It is essential in the design of a practitioner-research programme to acknowledge a number of challenges presented by the nature of the target group. By definition, those being recruited are already in employment, normally full time. Endemic to the enterprise, therefore, are the problems of balancing the demands of a full-time job with the need to maintain momentum on the research project. The features of such a situation include the following:

• defining an area of research activity exciting to the individual but sufficiently small in scale to be viable

- reserving and maintaining time for the research project against the immediate and apparently overriding pressures of the daily agenda
- separating and distinguishing the respective identities of practitioner and researcher
- acquiring the appropriate and necessary skills to function adequately in the researcher role
- confronting the ideological and logistical dilemmas of assessing practice which may have been directly delivered by the practitioner, certainly by the agency
- living with the ambivalence of colleagues who may be suspicious of the research function, and apprehensive as to its outcome
- preserving the integrity of the core research proposal against potentially shifting policy and practice priorities
- maintaining enthusiasm for the research enterprise and for the chosen design through inevitable setbacks, in an environment where others may as yet be indifferent
- bringing the piece of work to a successful conclusion, with a written account of the process in order that others can benefit.

Responses

Recruitment

Central to the aspirations for the practitioner-research programme was the desire to demystify the research process, to demonstrate that research activity was not the prerogative of those closeted in the ivory tower. At the same time, it was essential to acknowledge the distinct nature of research enquiry and to ensure that potential participants would be able to operate within a paradigm somewhat different to that of practice.

For the first round of recruitment, key individuals in each of the Scottish local authority social work departments were targeted and asked to circulate publicity material throughout the department. Notices were also placed in the professional journals. It was made clear that the target group was very much individuals engaged in direct practice who would be interested in evaluating an aspect of their own practice. This focus has perhaps somewhat relaxed over time to include wider aspects of agency practice, but the intent has remained that the participants should be primarily practitioners rather than those involved in a more senior management role. This would appear to contrast with the examples presented by other programmes, for example the MPhil/PhD by Practitioner Research in Social Policy offered by the then Cranfield Institute of Technology (Broad and Fletcher, 1993).

The fact that places on the programme for the first two years were free was, of course, a major incentive for authorities. On the other hand, agencies felt heavily committed to the training demands of community care implementation; indeed one local authority cited this as a higher priority. Nonetheless, even when, as for the third and fourth cohorts, agencies are required to make a contribution, it represents a major bargain at £350 (1994 prices) for a nine-month programme including six full days and three nights' accommodation.

Those interested in applying for a place on the programme are encouraged, indeed expected, to make contact with a member of the SWRC to discuss their proposed project. Following from such discussion, they submit a completed application form which includes an outline of the piece of research they wish to pursue.

The intention in selecting participants for the programme has always been to achieve a spread both between statutory and voluntary agencies and across regions. Working to total numbers of about twenty, the aim has been for perhaps five or six individuals from the voluntary sector and the remainder spread amongst the Scottish regions, but with some weighting to the larger authorities. Regions are invited to nominate their preferences when there are competing applications, but not all do so. One or two participants have been recruited from south of the border but in the main the assumption is of a Scottish focus.

At several points there have been difficult trade-offs between geographical spread and quality of the proposal. Ironically, the near-perfect proposal may well not be the most appropriate; if the individual is that competent perhaps the place should be allocated elsewhere. On the other hand proposals need to be viable; if the majority of those submitted from one region are fairly mediocre, does it reflect their actual quality or perhaps indicate that they were all produced at the last minute in a race against deadlines?

A deliberate attempt was made to screen out those who already appeared to have received a fair degree of research training. A postgraduate degree or experience as a research assistant would normally preclude selection. The aim was to target the genuinely 'naive researcher' motivated to acquire new skills.

In terms of motivation, those applying to the programme do so very much for the experience *per se*. There is no accreditation attached to the programme and participants receive no formal qualification. The issue of accreditation, for example by CCETSW, has been a difficult one. Apart from the lengthy process necessary in order to acquire accreditation, there was a concern that too formal a set of requirements would detract from the very individual experience that could be offered to each participant. Issues of comparability would come to the fore, and the opportunity for each to achieve on their own terms would be threatened. There might also be implications in terms of cost. The decision was reached in the short term, therefore, not to go down the accreditation route. It is difficult, however, to know how many potential participants have been dissuaded by this feature; by definition, only those prepared to accept the model are recruited.

Defining a project

For many of those applying for the practitioner-research programme, one of their earliest experiences must be of hearing their cherished research topic being ruthlessly hacked down in size. Indeed, one of the most crucial stages, hinted at in the initial telephone contact, but continuing during the drawing together of the research proposal, is the delimitation of a piece of work which both poses clear research questions and defines the research strategy through which they will be addressed. Such a strategy must be commensurate with the limited resources and timescale available to the participant.

It is the role of those presenting the programme within the Centre to enable individuals to transform their often wide-ranging interest into a feasible project. Some of this will occur during the initial enquiry stage, probing for clarity and for focus. More detailed definition will occur later during the initial study phase (see Chapter 3), when issues of focus and scale will be addressed in more detail.

A couple of examples may illustrate this process of reduction and redefinition, a process familiar to many in the research arena but of particular importance in the context of the participant relatively inexperienced in the research field. It is important for both the morale of the individual and for the credibility of the programme that the research projects that are attempted are commensurate with both the embryonic research skills of the individual and the limited time frame within which they can be conducted.

Initial enquiries, particularly from those who are project based, often speak generally of a desire to evaluate their particular initiative. Funding may specify that the project be evaluated, or the expectations of the current preoccupations with evaluation outlined at Chapter 1 may have generated an awareness of the activity. Such was the initial approach of Franki Campbell (1992) in relation to the Dundee Family Helper Scheme. She had been newly appointed as coordinator for a project designed to provide domiciliary support to individuals with mental health problems and was alert to the need for evaluation. Subsequent refinement led to specification of whose perspective was to be addressed in the evaluation and what aspects of service delivery were to be highlighted. A similar process of definition and specification refined the initial interest of Forsyth (1991) in aspects of specialist units within residential establishments to the detailed scrutiny of the perceptions of both staff and residents in relation to a particular dementia unit.

The hope and expectation was that the projects proposed would be those in which individuals themselves had a major interest and, indeed, stake. This was very much the case in the initial round, but subsequent years have seen at least one or two examples of projects generated primarily by the agency rather than the individual. The danger in these instances is that the agency may impose an excessively large agenda; for example, a participant from one authority found herself expected to address the entire region-wide system for assessing children and young people. A somewhat different experience was the apparent hijacking of a project part way through its development when the participant capitalized on the support which she had received to secure Scottish Office funding. A subsequent request by the programme organizers to see the project report which was met by a response referring to the need for clearance was a little difficult to swallow!

Management of limited time

Not unnaturally, those enrolling for the first round of the programme were anxious to know the likely time commitment required outwith the specific study periods. The initial estimate offered was in the region of a half-day per fortnight, and the hope was that participants' agencies would be sympathetic to such time being set aside. Feedback from the first intake (see below) suggested that in almost all cases this was an underestimate of the time required. Moreover, to talk in terms of individual days and half-days was less than helpful; operating in such a way meant valuable time was lost getting back into a project and input could feel disjointed and ineffective.

In subsequent years, emphasis has therefore been given to reserving blocks of time, allowing periods for concentrated input to the project. This is felt to be particularly important in the weeks immediately following the initial study period, allowing the project proposal to be put together before the initial enthusiasm and impetus has faded or is overtaken by the pressures of immediate service delivery. Likewise, if a block of time can be reserved at the analysis stage this can be of major benefit, focusing the mind on making sense of the data and reflecting on the conclusions that can be drawn. Beyond the first year, the recommended input has also been revised upwards to an average in the order of one day per fortnight.

Strategies for nurturing

As we wrote in a briefing note:

> we need to offer a unique blend of encouragement, practical assistance, realism and the 'human face of the ivory tower'.

Those with responsibility for the design and operation of this programme were determined to overcome the low completion rates highlighted earlier. Various devices designed to nurture and cajole were built into the structure. The need for such strategies was amplified by the uncertainty amongst many participants as to their ability to conduct 'proper research', their concerns that their sample was too small or their findings too insignificant to merit the description.

A key feature of the programme design is the opportunity for ongoing contact with the Centre. Following the initial three-day input, participants have their link with a Centre member. It has always been difficult to find an appropriate term for this relationship. The limited potential contact renders 'supervisor' a little heavy-handed, while 'mentor' perhaps invokes a somewhat different role model; 'advisor' has become the accepted label. Whatever the terminology, this contact is a crucial stopgap for those embarking on a process which is at the same time both strange and familiar: familiar in that many of the processes have their parallels in social work practice, strange in that different perspectives have to be adopted and techniques adapted (Whitaker and Archer, 1989).

There was some initial concern that the demands on the study advisors in the periods between the residential periods would be far in excess of the nominal five hours that had been specified. In practice, save for one or two individuals, this has proved more than adequate. For the majority, this contact tends to be by telephone, which perhaps acts in turn as a rationing device.

With a certain degree of trepidation, not least because of the terminology, participants in the first programme were introduced to the notion of a 'study buddy' (*sic*) and invited to sign up with a partner who would provide a contact point for mutual support and consolation during the life of the project. There was also some suggestion that partners could perhaps undertake research tasks on a reciprocal basis. This could assist, for example, where a practitioner was presented with the dilemma of interviewing their own clients.

The study buddy principle had a certain degree of success in the first year, although in practice it transformed into a couple of larger support groups. Meetings had a high social content and discussion specific to the programme was possibly at a fairly general level. Nonetheless, members of this cohort exhibited considerable solidarity and mutual empathy; most importantly, they delivered the goods! In the main, however, as evidenced by the responses of Table 2.1, participants are neutral with regard to having a study partner. It certainly does not appear to be the key feature to be pursued in a programme.

It is perhaps more difficult to generalize on the experience of working as a pair. In three of the four years to date, there has been an example of two people from the same agency working on the one study. Individual personalities and the vagaries of the particular research topic are both likely to influence the extent to which two heads add to a greater whole or merely tend to confusion. Certainly, however, where two people are involved it should prevent any shelving of activity – at least in theory!

At an apparently more superficial level, but in reality judged to be of major importance, is the attention given to nurturing participants during the two study periods. Little can be done about the basic nature of university student accommodation, but a special dinner, well lubricated, is included in each study period and a major effort is made to hold the participants as a group. All, on the total immersion principle, are expected to be residential, and Centre members are encouraged to remain with the group until the late evening. The experience is designed to be more for the participants than merely picking up a few handy hints on how to do a study. At its crudest, the intent is to generate a sense of commitment likely to ensure completion.

Structures and deadlines

Those participating in the programme are all professionals with busy practice lives. They have opted voluntarily for a programme whose reward is in the doing rather than in any qualification or certificate. This poses dilemmas as to the extent to which a rigid set of deadlines and demands can be exerted. Nonetheless, the inclination has been to be fairly ruthless in the imposition of routines and timetables, the argument presented being that this is very much in the longer-term interests of the individual. Indeed, it can be seen as a further facet of the nurturing approach outlined above. In practice, there may have been a tendency in the one-to-one relationship for the advisor to be less assertive, acknowledging perhaps that it was really up to the individual or, alternatively, uncomfortable with a more directive role.

The programme

Although the initial plans and costings allowed for the involvement of various outside contributors, the majority of the programme has been presented in-house. In the second and subsequent years, participants from the previous year have been invited back to 'tell it like it was', a highly valuable input for those beginning to feel daunted by what they have taken on. Prior to the initial meeting, all participants receive a copy of *Planning Investigative Projects: A Workbook for Social Services Practitioners*, devised by Carole Addison and published by the National Institute for Social Work in 1988.

The format for the two main study periods is presented in Figures 2.1

Figure 2.1 Programme for first study period.

Day one	
11.00–11.45 a.m.	Introductions
	Aims and expectations of course
11.45 a.m.–12.45 p.m.	Small groups to discuss individuals' topics
2.00–3.30 p.m.	Planning a study
	General research concepts
4.00–5.30 p.m.	Small-group exercises: collecting data
7.00–8.30 p.m.	Experiences of practitioner research (participants from previous year's programme)

Day two	
9.00–10.30 a.m.	Types and sources of data, methods of data collection
11.00 a.m.–12.30 p.m.	Writing a proposal – brief introduction to be followed by actual writing of broad outline of proposal to be put on display at 2 p.m.
2.00–4.00 p.m.	Small groups (3–4) in which participants present study plans to colleagues (study advisor in each group)
4.30–6.30 p.m.	Individual consultations with study advisor (one hour each)

Day three	
9.00–10.30 a.m.	Making sense of data – issues of analysis and presentation
	Exercises in groups
11.00 a.m.–1.00 p.m.	Individual consultations and private study
2.00–3.30 p.m.	Getting access and doing research in one's own agency

and 2.2, a format which has varied little over the four years. The remit for the first three days is demanding. Participants need to be introduced to basic principles of the research process, to be assisted in the formulation of research questions, and to be alerted to the various research techniques. There is a need both for fairly intensive teaching input and for the opportunity for more heuristic exploration of the research experience. A compromise has to be struck between providing sufficient of the basic building blocks and overloading the participant. Ideally, it could be argued, four or even five days might be a more realistic period for the necessary initiation into the research culture.

By the time they depart at the end of the first component, individuals will have had the opportunity to draw up the detail of their research proposal and to discuss it both with other participants and with the Centre staff member to whom they are linked. Following the presentation of a worked example, participants sit down to fill in a pro forma (Figure 2.3) for their own proposal. Again, the expectation that this be completed for display by the end of that session militates against any tendency to procrastinate. A date is given no more than two weeks hence

Figure 2.2   Programme for second study period.

Day one	
10.30 a.m.–12.30 p.m.	Introduction and presentations (20-minute presentations by individuals)
1.30–3.10 p.m.	Presentations (20-minute presentations by individuals)
3.30–5.00 p.m.	Dissemination strategies: discussion
5.00–7.30 p.m.	Individual meetings with study advisers
Day two	
9.30–11.10 a.m.	Presentations (20-minute presentations by individuals)
11.30 a.m.–12.30 p.m.	Presentations (20-minute presentations by individuals)
1.30–2.30 p.m.	Methodological reflections
	Small-group discussion based on participants' experiences of strengths and weaknesses of the research strategies and methods they have used
2.30–3.30 p.m.	Arrangements for finalizing reports and review of programme

by which the finalized proposals have to be submitted. Comments from participants leave no doubt that they find the initial study period, especially the first day, fairly exhausting. It is probably no less true for those delivering the programme!

As the timetable outlines, individuals are encouraged from an early stage to start talking about their planned project. The intention is that discussion over the three days should move back and forth between more general input on research design and methodology and the application of these general principles to their own example. At all stages the input is designed to stress the reality of the particular issue under discussion in the context of practitioner research. Thus, as will be demonstrated in Chapter 3, discussion of methods of data collection is firmly rooted in the practicalities of what can be achieved in the practitioner situation. Intimately related, routines presented for the analysis of data are not necessarily dependent on sophisticated technology.

The call-back day, some five months into the programme, provides an opportunity for participants to share their experiences to date and to start to turn their mind to some of the issues of analysis which may have passed them by at the first presentation. Individuals are reassured that others too have perhaps made less progress than they had hoped; at the same time, there is sufficient evidence of endeavour and progress to inspire individuals with renewed energy. In addition to sharing progress, participants receive some small group teaching on data analysis, revisiting, at a time when it is becoming more relevant, the basic principles outlined in the first study period.

Figure 2.3   Format for research proposal.

Title _____ Researcher _____
'Pair' _____
Aims (general)

Specific research questions

Methods (design; sample(s); data sources; procedure; methods; piloting)

Analysis

Access requirements

Estimated timetable

The second residential period (Figure 2.2) takes place nine months from the start of the programme. Prior to the final two-day study period participants are asked to send to their advisor an eight-page (maximum) preliminary report. Guidance suggests that this should include the following:

- the context of the research study and the research questions that were addressed (one page)
- the methodology adopted and brief details of how the study was carried out (two pages)
- the main findings that emerge from the initial analysis (four pages)
- the conclusions and recommendations planned to be drawn.

The hope is that by focusing on core findings there will be the opportunity for discussion and exploration of these before the final report is written. The majority of participants submit these preliminary reports.

All participants make a brief presentation as part of the final study period. SWRC members have found this a humbling experience, enjoying high-quality presentations across a range of different studies. Inevitably not all proposals have come to fruition in quite the way intended, while in other studies opportunities may have presented themselves that were not initially apparent.

The final study period also includes input from Centre members on the various stages and elements of dissemination. Individual achievements in this area are detailed in Chapter 5.

Beyond the final study period, the intention is that participants should submit some form of final report. The timescale here often tends to become a little fluid and should probably be tightened up. Nonetheless, as emphasized earlier, the large majority of studies have resulted in some form of final report. To date, volumes of summary reports have been produced for the first three years of the programme (SWRC, 1993, 1994).

Participant feedback

Participant evaluation of aspects of the programme has been sought on a number of occasions, including after each initial study period and at the end of the programme. In the main, such evaluations have been very favourable (Table 2.1 summarizes responses from the first three years of the programme). Individuals have generally been happy with, and appreciative of, the structure of the programme, the content of the study days, and the support received from the SWRC advisors, although there have been some requests for even clearer targets, deadlines and staging posts. There were also suggestions for adjustments to the tone and timing of the formal input to make it seem less daunting.

Table 2.1 Participants' evaluation of the programme (*n* = 45).

Comment	Strongly agree		Neutral	Strongly disagree	
	1	2	3	4	5
the course was interesting	36	9	–	–	–
the course was useful	32	12	–	–	–
the course was enjoyable	29	14	2	–	–
the course was helpful to my work	18	17	5	–	–
the course was a waste of time	–	–	–	1	43
I got sufficient support from my tutor	31	10	3	1	–
contact with other attenders was helpful	27	15	3	–	–
I would advise colleagues to attend such a course	31	14	–	–	–
a study partner was a worthwhile idea	9	7	21	5	1

In terms of actual content, however, participants were well satisfied. Nineteen of twenty respondents to a questionnaire on period one in the first year felt that the course achieved the correct balance between what was taught and what they already knew. This can be a very difficult balance to strike; the exclusion of those more experienced in research may have obviated too great a disparity. Some did, however, seek less didactic input, echoing the dilemma highlighted above. The mid-term 'call-back' day was valued as it provided contact, a boost to morale, and helped to keep the momentum going.

The problems that were reported were in several cases not within the direct control of the SWRC, although their occurrence could perhaps have been predicted. As noted above, virtually all those within the first cohort reported that the rough guideline of one day per month was an underestimate of the input that had been required and it was subsequently doubled. Not all, moreover, had the full-hearted support of their managers to working within core time. There was wide variation across a spectrum from those who had the autonomy to make the evaluative study central to their work activities to those who, either by overload or expediency, were in the main forced to rely on their own 'free time'. More practically, a few reported serious secretarial or administrative problems. Some would have welcomed unsolicited contact from advisors to jump them into action.

Some of the most interesting comments have reflected the perceptions held by practitioners. Individuals are, in the main, diffident as to their own skills and potential. They need to be reassured that what they are doing is worthwhile and that they are proceeding correctly. They need to be given the confidence to proceed, if necessary, to recognize that their first attempt at research may not necessarily be a perfect product. One participant drew an interesting contrast between their normal work mode and the process of doing research:

'Working alone on the research caused problems. I usually work as part of a social work team and part of an interdisciplinary team – so the lack of ongoing consultation and support and "handholding" was a problem!'

On the other hand, participants have expressed surprise that their results were so interesting and, in at least one case, that they had such an impact on the agency. For the organizers it was gratifying that the attention to the non-work components designed to generate enthusiasm and commitment appears to have paid off.

'Peer group was important! Interesting and also helped with motivation and continuation in the programme. "Care" by course staff – interest and enthusiasm and the dinners of course gave value to our efforts.'

We have dwelled at some length on what may strike as the relatively parochial detail of our own practitioner-research programme because there would appear to lie within it elements tending towards success. Having identified some of the problems for practitioners of pursuing the research paradigm, a programme was established designed to combat such problems. In Part Two, we proceed to the actual conduct of a piece of research. We do not aim to present an exhaustive account of all facets of the research process; there are a number of detailed sources for such technical information (see Appendix 2). What we regard as important is that practitioners have their attention drawn to key concepts, to particular ways of thinking, and to the range of analytical tools that are available. For those who wish to expand on the introductory concepts presented in the next chapter, we can make no better recommendation for an enjoyable read than the two volumes of Ford (1975), a methodological text unique in being genuinely entertaining.

Part Two

Concepts, strategies and methods for small-scale practice-based research

Chapter 3

Setting up a study

Reference has been made in Chapter 2 to the process of selecting a topic for research. In this chapter the options to be considered in the devising of the detailed research plan are explored. For the majority of practitioners, whatever the profession, the notion of research hovers as some ill-defined activity pursued by distant members of their professional group. Often the abilities ascribed to research are exaggerated; it is expected both to produce answers of an irrefutable certainty and to tackle questions that by the majority of those more closely involved in the research process would be deemed near impossible. A recent example that comes to mind is the request to carry out a detailed needs assessment within a particular locality to uncover the numbers of those with mental health problems who had also experienced sexual abuse.

Individuals can be unsure of the nature of the research exercise which they wish to undertake and uneasy about different areas of research activity – forms of evaluation, attempts at needs assessment, variants of audit or of monitoring. Aspirations are often unrealistic, not only in terms of certainty as highlighted above, but also with regard to the scale of activity that can be achieved within given timescales. The large majority of our own practitioners, for example, despite the initial discussion that may have taken place prior to enrolment on the course, arrive for the first three-day period with ideas which are at best embryonic and at times barely conceived.

Before launching into the design of a study, therefore, we believe it is important that the potential researcher is able to take a step back from the detailed conduct of the individual piece of research and place the potential enquiry within a wider context. We devote the first part of this chapter, therefore, to the clarification of a number of concepts which are key to an understanding of the research process. We detail five below:

- qualitative and quantitative research
- control groups
- sampling
- the user perspective
- pluralistic evaluation.

Our experience is that many practitioners find the exposition of these concepts valuable in demystifying the process, starting to break down possible misconceptions and uncertainties. Nothing can be more dispiriting than for the initial enthusiasm for research to be dispelled by inconsiderate lapses into research jargon. The selection of these particular concepts by no means implies that they are the only areas of importance; they do, however, address issues essential to placing a particular piece of research within a wider context. Moreover, they are regarded as the basic building blocks or pegs on which to hang the discussion of any potential piece of work.

Key research concepts

Qualitative and quantitative research

It is a firm belief of the authors that any absolute dichotomy of qualitative versus quantitative research is false. Nonetheless, it is necessary for those starting out in research to be aware of the particular attributes of each approach, to understand their strengths and weaknesses and to be familiar with the different methodologies which flow from the two ends of what could much more appropriately be viewed as a continuum.

It is often the case that the practitioner unfamiliar with the research world holds an impression that tends towards the more quantitative end of the research spectrum. The scientific method and the experimental tradition are more commonly part of taken-for-granted knowledge than the more detailed accounts of the qualitative investigator. In particular, practitioners may be familiar with exercises seeking to establish answers to questions of the form 'how many' or 'what types'. It is important, therefore, both to introduce practitioners to the various dichotomies that characterize this debate, for example 'hard' versus 'soft' data or numerical data-sets versus narrative accounts, and to warn against too ready an assumption that particular types of research activity automatically assume qualitative or quantitative outputs.

The quantitative approach often reflects a desire for large numbers to demonstrate with authority that particular patterns can be found. How many elderly people, for example, receive (or prefer) a particular set of services? Are patterns affected by fairly major variables such as an urban

Figure 3.1   Qualitative and quantitative approaches.

Qualitative   *Quantitative*

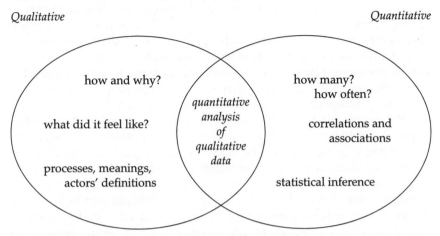

or rural location or the presence or absence of an informal carer? In order to provide anything resembling a definitive answer to such questions, a sufficiently large proportion of the population (see the discussion on sampling, below) have to be approached. Particular variables will be identified, for example, age, service receipt, location, caring network and the numbers falling into different categories for each variable will be accumulated.

A qualitative approach has less concern with absolute numbers; the interest is in gathering the attributions and experiences that may attach to particular variables. What is it like to live with or without a carer, what are the features of living in a rural location, what does it feel like to reach a particular age? Inevitably, such questions start to demand a more discursive approach, allowing for the complexities and uncertainties of meaning to emerge. The danger of simplification is underlined, however, if we cite the identification by Tesch (1990) of over forty different varieties of qualitative research. While some of these may hint of the semantic, there is obviously a need for the newly inducted researcher to steer a narrow course between excessive detail and oversimplification.

Although inevitably interlinked, it is difficult to separate the two approaches from the question of scale (Figure 3.1). There is a chicken-and-egg factor: qualitative work tends to be more exploratory, more in-depth, concerned with subjective experiences rather than the occurrence of discrete events. It therefore tends, often for pragmatic reasons, to work with smaller numbers. It is important to be able to make the correct judgements: when it is appropriate to go for the larger numbers required to give the authoritative overview, probably implying a more quantitative approach; when the detail of process or individual experience is more relevant and the requirement for more detailed exploration precludes, certainly for the practitioner–researcher, the involvement of large numbers.

Very often, once the purpose of a piece of research has been defined, decisions regarding the placing on the quantitative/qualitative continuum resolve themselves. Moreover, as will be pursued in Chapter 4, the placing on the continuum tends to determine in turn, at least in part, the particular research techniques that will be employed. There does not necessarily, however, have to be a choice between the more quantitative and the more qualitative. For example, a survey of a considerable number of people could be undertaken to derive baseline numbers and responses on key items; this could then be followed by more detailed, more qualitative interviews, with a smaller number of individuals.

It is the case in social work that potential research topics are often associated with relatively small numbers, for example pilot schemes or the small-scale interventions which frequently characterize the organization of social work. Moreover, people often wish to get at the detail of what is happening, to seek to understand specific situations or particular responses. Again, this tends to lead to the more qualitative end of the scale, a tendency supported also by Addison (1988).

Control groups

A common concern of the practitioner newly approaching research is 'will I need a control group?' Often this is asked with little knowledge of what the control group might entail and why indeed its use might be desirable. Again, however, it reflects some hazy image of what research should be about, derived from the scientific tradition. The nature of the research situations that occur in social work and social welfare determine that very often the answer to the question will be no. Sheer practicalities often foreclose on more sophisticated debate on the relative merits of opposing research paradigms.

The presence of a control group implies a piece of research conducted within the paradigm of the experimental design. Central to such a design is a concern to attribute causality. One group, the experimental group, receive a certain intervention (traditionally the 'drug'), while a second group, otherwise similar in all respects, receives no intervention (or the 'placebo'). Any effects of the intervention are then measured through the comparison of specified outcomes for the two groups. More sophisticated versions of the control group concept lead to withdrawal of the intervention followed by a second introduction or similar variants.

It has to be questioned, however, whether the interventions of much of social work are of this type. How often is it either (a) possible and (b) ethical to allocate certain individuals to receive a service and others to remain without. Moreover, it could be argued that the exact nature of the social work intervention is much more difficult to specify than the pharmacology of the drug capsule. Elements of support, the components of counselling or, more prosaically, the routines of the review process are not readily reduced to a simple formula defining a key structure.

The term 'control group' implies an active process of allocation to either the experimental or control group which can be problematic for social welfare. More often, it can be feasible to achieve a comparison group, individuals from the same or similar setting matched on key features (variables) with those subject to the experimental intervention. In the context, for example, of elderly people discharged from hospital, the variables to be controlled (and therefore matched on) might be age, gender and some measure of physical dependency and/or social functioning. It may also be the case that rather than proactively creating the experimental situation, the researcher takes advantage, often retrospectively, of a naturally occurring experiment, referred to in research terminology as the 'quasi-experimental design'.

A particular variant of the experimental design which we have always felt might appeal to the practitioner–researcher on the grounds of scale and access is the single-case experiment – although it has to be said that we have no examples to date from our own programme. Under this model, the focus is on the effects of intervention in a single case, with periods of intervention alternating with reversion to the baseline norm. Outcomes appropriate to the subject under scrutiny are defined. Commonly cited examples of this device often relate to truancy, observing the effects of varying interventions on the truancy record of the individual, or to bedwetting. For those interested in pursuing experimental designs further, an excellent exposition can be found in Robson (1993).

The experimental design is often associated with a 'hypothesis-testing' approach. As with other terms which have migrated from their technical base to a more generic lay usage, it can be difficult to reclaim the initial meaning of the term 'hypothesis'. It is essential, we would argue, that there is a clear understanding of fundamental concepts such as this. Clarity of definition and the use, wherever possible, of terminology which has universal understanding can only assist in the drive to extend research-mindedness amongst a wider network. A hypothesis, therefore, should be a statement of the relationship between specific events or processes, cast in a form which can be tested. An example could be, 'people who attend regular groupwork will demonstrate improved social skills outside the group . . .' In its strongest form, the hypothesis is framed in terms such that the investigation seeks to demonstrate the truth, or otherwise, of a particular assertion as to the relationship between specific events through the use of the control or comparison group. Thus the hypothesis would predict significant differences between the two groups; the null hypothesis, conversely, predicts that there will be no such differences.

As with the qualitative/quantitative dichotomy, it is only fair to point out that in the messy, real world the debates around these concepts can be much more contentious. Many involved in scientific endeavour would challenge too rigid an interpretation of the demands of the scientific model as outlined above, and would wish to allow for the uncertainty and exploration which is a necessary part of the scientific advance. It is essential, nonetheless, to understand any concept before one can disaggregate it. For the practitioner–researcher in particular, fluency in the key concepts provides the solid grounding from which such debates can be pursued. At this stage, therefore, it is not unduly simplistic to associate the use of control groups and hypothesis testing with the more positivistic, deductive type of endeavour, and to contrast it with the hypothesis-generating type of activity characteristic of the more interpretative, qualitative tradition.

Sampling

Closely lapping control groups and hypotheses in the concerns of the would-be researcher are the perceived complexities of sampling. Again, this is a concept which has strayed into everyday parlance and may therefore already hold a definition for the practitioner. It is not, however, a complex concept to understand; it is the attainment of the desired sample that most often is problematic.

The notion of sampling addresses the question of how to select the subjects to be studied from the total number of such cases or individuals that exist (termed the 'population'). The motivation is very practical – to reduce the number of respondents that have to be sought. A concern with representativeness may also underlie the process; the components of the sample will be selected from the population in a manner that ensures that the sample replicates the population on certain key dimensions. Thus, if what is required is a selection from the total population of the phenomenon under scrutiny, instances should be selected in a manner designed to produce a representative subset of the total. Such is the standard random sample whereby the selection procedure gives each case an equal likelihood of being selected for inclusion within the sample. Provided there are sufficient numbers within the sample, the logic is that one should be able to extrapolate from the sample to the population. The assumption is that the findings for the sample hold true for the population as a whole. Techniques for selecting a random sample are increasingly familiar with the spread of 'lottery fever', and can range from the traditional drawing of names from a hat, to the use of random number tables or the more sophisticated computerized equivalent.

Beyond the random sample lie various sampling devices to control more precisely the elements of a population which should be drawn into the sample. Such a process is termed 'stratification'. In place, for example, of the completely random sample of community care cases from a particular region, there may be the desire to ensure that representatives of different care groups are included. Thus, the intention may be to select eighty cases but for these to be stratified into twenty each of elderly people, individuals with mental health problems, with learning disability and with physical disability. Alternatively, it could be that the stratification which is desired is by geographical area, or by length of contact, or by age of the individual. If the numbers in each group or stratum are selected according to the numbers in the total population it can be termed 'proportionate stratified sampling'; if the weighting is unequal, perhaps because a particular interest in one group leads to a desire to 'oversample', the appropriate description is disproportionate stratified sampling.

A variety of other ways exist of dividing the total population for sampling purposes. Systematic sampling involves the selection by random means of the initial case for the sample, but with others being selected according to some fixed interval. There might, for example, be a register listing certain types of cases which for the purposes of sample selection have been numbered in sequence. The initial starting point is determined and then every subsequent fifth or tenth or whatever case is added to the sample. If such a mechanism is to be adopted it is essential that there is no prior ordering within the list otherwise the sample will become skewed. Often there may be histories to the construction of lists which lead to unintended consequences in the selection of cases. This strategy should only be applied therefore where there can be certainty that distortion will not occur.

Different types of sampling	• random • stratified • systematic • cluster • multistage • quota • convenience • purposive • snowball

A device termed 'cluster sampling' is often adopted for practical reasons, for example to facilitate, in an interview study, accessibility. The total population is divided into a number of groupings or clusters, most simply perhaps on the basis of geographical area. A subset of the total number of clusters is then selected. A sequence of sampling decisions may be involved, characteristic of multistage sampling. Thus, certain regions may be selected, certain districts within those regions, certain teams within those districts, and finally certain individuals from the specific teams.

Although these different variants of sampling can fascinate, the most common question asked with regard to sampling is how many instances are required – how many are enough? Although there are complex formulae from which an answer to this question can be created, it is more realistic to suggest that it depends on the circumstances of the particular study, on the questions that it is intended to ask, on the particular analysis it is hoped to perform, and on the purpose for which the enquiry is being carried out. The studies of the practitioner are often exploratory, testing feasibility or clarifying research questions. It may, therefore, be less important to scrutinize 'power tables' designed to indicate the minimum number required in a sample, than to ensure that a thorough understanding of the phenomenon under scrutiny avoids silly questions being asked or spurious conclusions being drawn. Indeed, both authors have to confess, somewhat shamefacedly, that in the course of lengthy research careers they have never actually employed these elusive tables.

The strategy outlined above is most accurately termed 'probability sampling', it being possible to specify the probability of selection for each instance within the population. It is probably true to say that the research of the practitioner is rarely likely to fully satisfy this requirement and is often more accurately characterized as non-probability sampling. Not least, this may be because it is difficult to obtain the listing of the total population involved and an appropriate sampling frame is therefore absent.

Much more relevant to the practitioner–researcher, therefore, are strategies which relax the requirements of representativeness. In quota sampling, for example, researchers seek to select cases to fill predetermined quotas set on certain key dimensions. It may be, for example, that a number of residential homes are to be visited and interviews achieved with a certain number of individuals scoring within a set range on a dependency measure. Provided that particular criteria are met, it does not matter which specific individuals are selected.

Other sampling devices rely heavily on pragmatism. The term 'convenience sampling' reveals the practicality of drawing upon available cases or individuals for investigation of the particular questions under discussion. 'Purposive sampling' suggests a somewhat more guided selection, a sample being drawn and perhaps extended in accord with emergent and developing ideas around a topic. Such an approach may or may not involve an element of 'snowball sampling', most commonly used when seeking interview respondents and involving the building up of a network of informants from a small number of initial contacts.

It should not, however, be the lot of the practitioner–researcher, any more than the more general social welfare researcher, to feel that the sampling devices they can adopt are in some way inferior. Rather, the necessity is for a clear understanding of what can be concluded from the sample under scrutiny, the extent to which the account is of a set of particular individuals, the extent to which it is appropriate to draw out generalizations.

User perspective

The fourth research concept we have chosen to highlight is the user perspective (see, for example, Sainsbury, 1987; Harding and Upton, 1991). The changing terminology employed to refer to those in receipt of social welfare services is itself an interesting study. Current consensus tends to lie with 'user', although there is some unease as to the transferability of the term outwith the United Kingdom due to analogies with substance use.

There should be little argument with the assertion that details of the user response are essential if a service is to be effective and accountable. Increasingly, attention to the user voice has become a part of the rhetoric of both central and local policy documents. At a practice level this has led to the careful development of initiatives designed to both ascertain and incorporate such responses (for a comprehensive listing in relation to one area see Black, 1992).

Exploration of the user perspective often holds a particular attraction for the practitioner–researcher. Extensive experience of delivering services may have provoked an interest in how such delivery is experienced by those on the receiving end; likewise, anxiety as to the effectiveness of intervention may produce a desire to explore more deeply with recipients whether the workers' efforts have any impact. The practitioner–researcher may also feel at ease with the practicalities of seeking out the user perspective, well equipped with the necessary interview skills. In other words, the activity itself may not feel too alien from the familiar work routines, particularly in comparison with perhaps more esoteric research methodologies.

Given the widespread enthusiasm for exploration of the user perspective, it is perhaps appropriate to sound a few notes of caution. Firstly, exhortations to pay heed to the user can be very much a political expedient – part of the wider consumer rhetoric of charters and complaints procedures and choice. There may be a directive to ensure that the user perspective is given sufficient priority. But this can sometimes assume that there is a single user perspective, that a unitary response can be neatly packaged and incorporated into appropriate planning or review structures. In reality, of course, users are no different from professional groups; there are a multiplicity of user views whose variance and diversity must not be compromised. To crudely characterize *the* user perspective is therefore unwise.

The second warning to the practitioner–researcher on the user perspective is to think carefully about the research strategies through which it is to be gathered. Research evidence suggests (Gutek, 1978) that whether it be home-care services or probation or indeed washing-up liquid, crude enquiries as to the level of satisfaction will generate positive responses in the order of 80 per cent. In research carried out by one of the authors on the parental perspective on the children's hearings system (Petch, 1988), 80 per cent of parents did indeed say that they were satisfied with the actual disposal that their child received. Behind that satisfaction with the specific outcome, however, lay a whole range of detailed joys, dissatisfactions, criticisms and suggestions. It is therefore essential, we would argue, that the user perspective is sought through research instruments and methodologies sufficiently sensitive to counteract this tendency to broad statements of compliance.

The user perspective, therefore, is most readily sought through the direct face-to-face interview which allows for the teasing out of the detailed response, and for the exploration with the interviewer of potentially conflicting responses and sentiments over time. This is not, however, entirely to exclude alternative, more structured techniques. Often the choice will depend on the existing knowledge. If there has already been preliminary work to assist in the drawing up of detailed questions it may be possible to go for a more structured approach, possibly a questionnaire; if the focus is very much on exploration of a new area, the tendency should be to prefer the opportunity for the greater depth offered by the exploratory interview.

Pluralistic evaluation

Consideration of the user perspective leads neatly to the fifth and final of the common research concepts to which we consider the practitioner–researcher should be alert. The notion of pluralistic evaluation has been most neatly discussed and given the label by Smith and Cantley (1984, 1985), although others would assert that they too developed a similar line of argument.

Pluralistic evaluation allows a recognition that different parties or stakeholders in any arena may have very different notions of a successful outcome. Rather than treating such diversity as problematic, pluralistic evaluation acknowledges, indeed gives central place to, the varying perspectives proffered by different parties within a particular process or initiative.

Looking at a programme for hospital closure, for example, the individual service user may be primarily concerned with access to alternative accommodation and the quality of life associated with that new setting. Those concerned with service planning may be looking for a swift reduction in bed numbers and for the achievement of savings targets. Hospital management may be anxious that the closure is achieved without any untoward publicity featuring individual incidents. Key workers may look for success in the extent to which different agencies collaborate in providing an integrated service to meet the needs of the individual. Carers may wish their fears allayed that the care on offer is inferior to that which they themselves can provide. The list could be extended to include others associated with the hospital closure and for each group their particular notions of a successful outcome and the means by which this should be measured could be highlighted. Suffice to emphasize that pluralistic evaluation gives explicit recognition to the often very different priorities of health board, social work manager, front-line worker, voluntary agency, carer and individual user, actively seeking out and detailing at least some of the different perspectives.

Practitioners may be implicitly aware of the different agendas and different priorities lurking behind a particular initiative. Often, however, there has not been open acknowledgement of this dilemma. It can, therefore, be refreshing for the practitioner as they embark on research to bring such awareness to the fore. The identification and specification of the plurality of perspectives that intrude into any endeavour starts a process of evaluation which, even if the decision is to concentrate on a limited range of those perspectives, has alerted the researcher to the messy real world. The particular sets of objectives with which one is working are made explicit.

The interest of taking into account a plurality of definitions of effectiveness, as well as the dangers of not doing so, were illustrated by Cornish's (1991) study of the operation of a multidisciplinary unit for children and young people at risk of school exclusion. Having identified a range of objectives for the young people following referral to the unit, Cornish asked four different parties to rate on a four-point scale the success with which they had been pursued with each member of a sample of ten: the young person, their parents, an education linkworker and a keyworker. While there was limited but not total agreement as to what the objectives were, Cornish found that there was not a single instance of four-way agreement about 'success', and several of diametrically opposed assessments. There is therefore a cautionary tale for researchers here, as well as a finding which points up differences in perspective, of considerable relevance to service development, both between clients and workers, and between workers of different disciplines.

Once the area for investigation has been tied down, one of the most important stages of the research process is the development of a set of researchable questions. For those working in certain traditions this would be equated, as outlined above, with the definition of a hypothesis; we prefer to work more broadly with the notion of a set of questions which are going to direct both the scope and the methodology of the investigation (but see Black (1993) for a fuller discussion).

Defining research questions

The art of defining specific research questions is one of moving from the general statement of interest or purpose to the particular set of questions which themselves define what data is to be collected. They must therefore be researchable questions and not rhetorical; in other words, they must be questions that are capable of being answered by empirical data. Alongside this is the question of feasibility. There is little point in having good researchable questions if, for example, there are serious difficulties in contacting the sample which would be needed to answer them, as might be the case with studies of services to mobile populations. Alternatively, it would be foolish for reseachers to embark on a study requiring particular language skills or modes of communication with which they are unfamiliar.

A first attempt at defining a question often produces something along the lines of 'how can we improve services for people with dementia?' This is not a *research* question, in the sense that the issue of what action to take cannot be settled by empirical research; it may form part of the conclusions which might be drawn from a study of services to people with dementia, but such a study would have set itself (properly) a series of rather different questions.

A second attempt at arriving at a research question, therefore, might be 'how successful are current services at meeting the needs of people with dementia?' This is an improvement and could serve as a statement of a general aim for a study, but still does not take us very far. Do we assume that we know what the needs of people with dementia are, say from previous research or from textbook wisdom? Are we talking of all people with dementia, or, say, of elderly clients already known to the agency? Or people with severe dementia? Are we really talking about sufferers themselves, or also their carers? Are we talking about all their needs, or only some of them? What might we mean by 'successful'?

These are the kinds of reflection which need to take place before a set of researchable questions can be arrived at. If circumstances permit, it is desirable if at this point the researcher consults relevant literature to see what (if any) work has been previously done and to establish what might be regarded as known and what questions previous research has left unanswered. This would especially be the case if the initial interest is articulated in the context of a particular service such as an innovatory day-care scheme for people with dementia.

Readers may wonder why we have not made more up to this point o the role of the literature. While we do not wish to dismiss the importance of seeking out other studies within the area chosen by the practitioner, not least if there have been significant classics, we consider it important that the practitioner does not become swamped in the early stages. Student theses often demonstrate a tendency to overdose on the literature at the expense of original empirical study; the practitioner should not be similarly diverted. Moreover, it may often be the case that the more interesting studies, particularly of recent phenomena, are as yet of limited circulation and not readily available to those with limited access to libraries or other literature sources.

A number of different kinds of study could follow from the initial interest in services to people with dementia outlined above. One might tackle questions such as:

- How many of our current elderly clients have dementia in mild, moderate or severe forms?
- How does this compare with estimates of the number of elderly people in the population who have dementia?
- How many of them have a carer who is normally available for support?
- What services are they receiving?

This would result in a quantitative and descriptive study, of rather a simple kind in terms of design, and the researcher will already be thinking about potential sources of data and methods of collecting it. Its results, perhaps not especially 'interesting' in themselves, could feed into a debate about the 'success' of existing services in reaching people with dementia.

It would, however, say little about the quality of existing provisions. A second approach looking at quality through the perceptions of users and professionals might be to take a rather different set of questions:

- What (if anything) do elderly people with dementia, known to the agency, say they would like from social work?
- What do their carers say they would like for the person with dementia?
- What do carers say they would like for themselves?
- What do their social workers say that they need?
- What services are they currently receiving?
- How 'satisfied' are elderly people with dementia and their carers with different aspects of what they are receiving?
- Has their quality of life as measured by a standard scale improved following service provision?
- How do professionals assess the degree of improvement in the clients' and carers' quality of life following service provision?

These questions could be further refined, for example by specifying how to be measured, but would serve as a starting point for .udy. As the researcher is mulling over the potential ques- y be addressed, consideration will be given to qualitative or methods, sample size, control or comparison groups, and a gistical matters. Are all these questions in principle and in pr... swerable, and by what kinds of data or method? Is an appropriate sample available? How many of the questions may be undertaken with the resources available? The researcher may reluctantly decide that some may have to be omitted.

It is usually appropriate to start with perhaps four to six specific questions of the kind outlined above. As well as a shift from the general to the particular in this process, there is a cognate movement from the 'interesting' to the feasible. It is of course preferable if the researcher has a live interest in the topic to start with, and if that interest can survive the sometimes rather ruthless pruning of scope that often accompanies the refining process. In the first place, the researcher has an inclusive approach, as reflection opens up a whole range of interesting topics. Eventually, for the sake of doing a clean job, the researcher arrives at an exclusive set of questions.

Checklist for research questions	• are they jargon-free? • are they specific, concrete, down to earth? • does each question focus on a single aspect of the topic? • are they measurable? • can you specify the kinds of data that you will need to answer them? • are the data available or accessible?

Answering the questions

The potential researcher can be overwhelmed by the apparent number of decisions which clamour to be made as a piece of research is contemplated. Very often, however, such decisions are each contingent to a large extent on others: once initial choices have been made, an unfolding sequence slots into place. While this may reduce the complexity of the process, it does underlie the importance of making appropriate choices in the early stages.

In deciding how to design an investigation to answer the research questions that have been posed, the major decisions that have to be made focus on the research strategy to be embraced, the methods to be selected and the analysis to be pursued (these are addressed in Chapter 4), closely followed by the negotiations for access and the timetable to be adopted (see Figure 2.3 on p. 27). In devising the research strategy and selecting the associated techniques, decisions should take account of the key concepts outlined above. Examining these in conjunction with the researchable questions, very often a preferred design fairly readily emerges.

Particular care is necessary in prospective studies when trying to estimate the rate of referrals, in order, for example, to determine how long it may take to accumulate a sample of 50. Experience shows that practitioners frequently overestimate the flow, and that researchers collude with them only too readily to maximize numbers of cases in their sample. A good rule of thumb is to multiply by at least two the estimated time to reach the required target: it can almost be guaranteed that as soon as a researcher appears, new cases will mysteriously dry up.

Negotiating access

The practitioner has a major advantage over other researchers in that the lengthy process of negotiation for access which characterizes, often indeed comes to dominate, other studies is usually not necessary. Even when some element of negotiation is required, it is usually within a familiar system and with colleagues from whom one can hope for a certain degree of cooperation and encouragement. While this should not be taken for granted – certain investigations may provoke anxieties notwithstanding their internal nature – normally it gives the practitioner researcher an important headstart. An in-house researcher, for example, may have ready access to case files or policy documents denied to the external researcher, or only made available after lengthy justification and negotiation.

Although doors may open more readily for the practitioner–researcher, this brings with it a particular need for clarity. For their own peace of mind, the practitioner needs to be clear about the definition of the research being undertaken and who is in the driving seat. There may be strong pressure to undertake a piece of research consistent with an agency agenda; alternatively, investigation of areas considered weaker or in other ways problematic may be discouraged. Our strong recommendation is that the practitioner should feel that the specification and direction of the piece of research is theirs; it is very much easier to remain committed through the inevitable setbacks when there is a sense of ownership over the focus and design of the investigation. Moreover, the practitioner–researcher should resist attempts to hijack studies for the agency's own ends; very often the scale and focus of the study is thereby changed, to the detriment of the practitioner's own ideas. There will be occasions, however, when researchers find themselves taking on prior agreements in terms, say, of how the research will be disseminated or what arrangements for the clearance of results will be required. Again we would recommend caution in terms of too ready compliance with conditions that may become burdensome at a later stage.

It is also necessary to be clear, as prefaced in Chapter 1, about the particular and different identity of the researcher as opposed to the practitioner. In terms of skills, for the social work researcher more than for others, there is an apparent congruence, particularly with regard to interviewing. This only increases the importance of the practitioner clearly identifying with their research role, adjusting their perspective for example from one of intervention to one of evaluation.

Adopting such a perspective in one's own workplace is not always unproblematic. Working in a different relationship to work colleagues may generate some degree of suspicion and anxiety on their part. Situations may arise where details are obtained of colleagues' work which raise doubts as to its quality; occasionally examples of bad practice may be revealed. The practitioner–researcher has to decide in such circumstances when to take further action and when to let the evidence rest as research data.

There may be a number of more pragmatic issues concerned with the development of access. Certain agencies operate their own screening devices for intended research within their area. Although these may systematically be applied to researchers outwith the agency, there may be rather more discretion as to the rigidity with which they are applied in-house. Whatever their location, all potential researchers should be aware of the various codes of ethics to which researchers work. Some agencies may have developed these in-house; others will adopt the general principles outlined by, for example, the Social Research Association or the Social Services Research Group. Common elements, however, will address the need for confidentiality with regard to the storage and disclosure of data, including anonymity in published reports, and the need for respondents to give informed consent. In particular circumstances, most usually when a health population is required, the research proposal will have to be screened by the local medical ethics committee.

The presence of departmental routines for research access should not always be seen as an additional hurdle. Their existence may well demonstrate the presence of an in-house research function which may be able to offer both valuable moral support and practical assistance, for example by way of computing facilities, to the putative researcher. The need one to fulfil the support and sounding-board function should derestimated. Considered a critical component of the Stirling e, lone researchers within agencies should seek to find their own substitute. Support is required at many stages of research, be it sympathetic and encouraging during the initial setbacks and modifications, to the more challenging input necessary at the stage of analysis when it is helpful for initial conclusions to be scrutinized and extended. Our experience, however, both on the programme and elsewhere, would suggest that support is particularly useful at the early and late stages; during the data-collection phase many of the earlier problems will have been solved and the process can be more routine. The benefit of support from someone familiar with the vagaries of the research process itself rather than just the technical mechanics cannot be underestimated. The empathy of those who have experienced research traumas is invaluable.

Working with colleagues

We have referred at a number of points to potential dilemmas unique to the practitioner–researcher for whom work colleagues may variously (and simultaneously) be cast in the role of research subject, critic, co-investigator, sceptic or conscript. To some extent, the practitioner–researcher must be proactive, have antennae alert for potential hostility and be willing to provide the explanations and reassurances that should allay unwarranted fears. It may also be necessary, ironically perhaps at a stage when the researcher feels least confident, to adopt an informed and assertive manner which carries others forward with enthusiasm. But perhaps most important is a basic attitude of honesty and openness towards colleagues, a commitment to keep them in touch and informed as to the progress of the research, accompanied by the sensitivity to remain quiet if a danger of research-talk overload is sensed. Any researcher, but not least the practitioner–researcher, is well advised to cultivate an attitude of modesty rather than arrogance in their research demeanour.

Timescale

The nagging of colleagues in the workplace may be an unintentional blessing; expectations have been raised and the product must therefore be delivered. The task of the practitioner–researcher is eased if a realistic timetable is devised. This must be adequate to allow for the development and completion of the work, but should not extend indefinitely. An underlying assumption of practitioner research is that the scale of the enterprise is modest, with empirical work commensurate with the resources available. Occasionally, the practitioner may enlist a colleague or other co-worker to assist, particularly, for example, to increase the number of interviews attained or to avoid direct contact by practitioner–researchers with their own clients. As with any research proposal, it is essential that the design allows adequate time both at the early stages of development and during the later phase of the research when results are starting to emerge. The more that early findings can be exposed to outside scrutiny, the more robust they are likely to become through challenge and refinement.

There is perhaps an inherent dilemma with regard to timescale. On the one hand it could be argued that there is a natural momentum to a piece of research, perhaps longer than three months but less than two years. On the other hand, as argued in Part One, there is a desire to promote research-mindedness, for research thinking and indeed activity to become routine and routinized. The one implies a time-limited venture; the other is an argument for the incorporation of particular monitoring or evaluation activities into long-term practice. Thus, for example, the use of individualized objectives to map progress, initially developed as practitioner research, becomes a part of the regular review process (Cornish, 1991). Research instruments become review documents.

We turn now, in the following chapter, to explore the selection and development of such research instruments. As with the research concepts outlined above, the treatment is illuminative rather than exhaustive. Texts to which reference can be made include Herbert (1990), Robson (1993), Edwards and Talbot (1994) and Phillips *et al.* (1994).

Chapter 4

The methodological repertoire

There is no theoretical reason to exclude any data-collection technique from the repertoire of the practitioner–researcher; there are often, however, practical reasons which restrict the choices that can be made. In this discussion of the range of methods, we will draw liberally on examples of the specific techniques employed in the studies pursued by the practitioners on our own course.

Whatever the technique adopted, the purpose of it is to gather the data which will assist in the answering of the research questions identified at Chapter 3. Data can come in many forms and many degrees of structure. People sometimes speak of research 'data' as if it were a commodity, existing 'out there' and waiting to be 'gathered' by the researcher. This is misleading. Data is the product of data-collection procedures, and exists only in the context of these procedures which are determined by the purposes of a particular study; the form it takes depends on the precise way in which researchers formulate their questions or other data-gathering devices.

Before we examine the potential ways of collecting data, the preliminary point needs to be made that data may be gathered in a relatively *structured* or a relatively *unstructured* form. Tightly structured data might be obtained from a question where respondents are invited to tick one of several alternative categories specified by the researcher. Unstructured data are produced by an open-ended question to which respondents write or speak an answer in their own words and at whatever length they choose. These are two ends of a spectrum with various intermediate points.

Choice between options here will be influenced in part by the topic and context, and one research instrument is likely to include both structured and unstructured questions. Researchers need to bear in mind, however, that there are considerable implications for analysis. Unstructured data will require substantial investment of time and effort before it can be fully interpreted. We will explore in this chapter the different techniques which can be employed to gather in the data necessary for the response to the research questions.

Strategies for data collection	<ul><li>analysis of secondary sources</li><li>monitoring devices</li><li>questionnaires</li><li>interviews</li><li>scales and schedules</li><li>observation</li><li>diaries</li></ul>

It may be appropriate at this stage to enter a word of caution concerning accounts to be found elsewhere of how research is done. Research textbooks often adopt a tone which suggests a perfection and purity in the research process rarely, we would argue, to be found in the real world. Two major sets of factors intervene. The first, to which the social welfare researcher may be particularly prone, are the vagaries of respondent behaviour. Individuals lose questionnaires, fail to accord with the categories of schedules, walk out of interviews, refuse to be observed, or wander off the subject, however assertive the interviewer. The second set of factors relate more directly to the researchers themselves. Whether it be the relatively trivial – three pencils did actually all break, the prompt cards were left at the previous interview – or the more substantial, researchers, no less than others, are guilty of human error. An important flaw in the wording of an interview schedule was not spotted until long past the pilot stage ('are you better off?' – *not* intending a monetary association), distribution addresses were not retained for follow-up letters, the interviewer lost control of the interview and allowed the respondent to wander way beyond the remit. More prosaically, a particular piece of research became tedious, even wearisome.

The authors support strongly the tradition initiated by the classic accounts collected by Bell and Newby (1977), Bell and Encel (1978) and Bell and Roberts (1984) of 'telling it as it really is'. We consider such accounts are particularly helpful to the relatively new researcher who may be intimidated by the presumptions of perfection recounted elsewhere. We accept, however, that it may be necessary for researchers to have attained a certain degree of confidence in their own abilities before they feel able to be completely frank as to both the natural reality and their own lapses. Most recently, and of particular relevance to our own field, Shakespeare *et al.* (1993) have edited a fascinating collection of accounts by researchers reflecting with honesty on the various stages of the research process.

Secondary sources

It should not be assumed that researchers always have to create their data source from scratch. There are a range of secondary sources which can be accessed, for some of which the practitioner–researcher may have a natural advantage. Secondary sources range across the set of agendas for the meetings of a voluntary organization, the committee meeting minutes of the local authority, published and unpublished census data and the policy papers produced in the formulation of new guidance in a particular arena.

Of particular significance in the current context, however, are the various case records, social enquiry reports and such like which form the substance of social work files. Practitioner researchers may well be able to gain privileged access to such records, access which may not be afforded to an outsider; they will certainly be aware of the constraints under which they are produced and the potential pitfalls.

Case records embrace the range of documentation prepared for any case, including routine case file recordings, social background reports and reports prepared by specialist third parties. Such records can offer considerable material without necessarily a great expenditure of effort for its collection. Thus, it may be possible to extract details of the number of contacts between different individuals or agencies, the progress achieved towards specific objectives, or the motivation behind particular strategies.

In the ready availability of case records, however, lies also their major weakness: for case records were not created with research as the primary aim. In many instances, therefore, the data they may yield is at best an approximation and at worst inadequate. It is obviously a fallacy to extract as a significant variable the number of visits that were made in connection with a case if there was no requirement to record every visit. Likewise, records may be geared towards the recording of the negative (or positive) and may therefore offer a biased account. And there is the larger question of the ways in which records may be constructed so as to provide a justification for the action taken against the possibility of inspection of files by supervisors. The use of case records must therefore be treated with caution; it is a second-order analysis of data which is already a selected record of the incident or activity under scrutiny.

A more mundane consideration in the use of case records is their quality. Social work recording is the butt of many jokes which are no doubt equally or even more appropriately directed towards other professionals. Nonetheless, it is unwise without prior confirmation of their coverage or accuracy to plan a piece of research entirely dependent on this resource.

Often the researcher will have to devise an additional recording device to accumulate the relevant pieces of data that are being extracted from records. At its most basic this might take the form of a grid tallying the number of contacts that were made with various professionals. A more sophisticated reading of records might attempt to extract details of the needs that were being identified in different cases. Whatever the complexity, however, the researcher should be aware that in the process of translating information from the case records into entries on the recording device, they are imposing their own interpretative framework. This may be minimal – for example, whether to record the specific number of contacts or to group into bands, 1–5, 6–10 etc. – or more extensive – assigning to summary categories the varied objectives that might be stated for specific cases. This need to translate the complex record into a simpler summary is also, however, an asset. In effect, one is carrying out the first stage of the analysis process, reducing a large amount of data to a more manageable and classified form. Though it may seem a betrayal, indeed a waste, of the fine detail to present it in summary form, this indeed is the first stage towards making the generalizations that constitute research findings.

A number of examples will illustrate the potential. The second example, of perinatal risk indicators, exemplifies a common problem when more than one set of records is involved. Names may change, the lead person on file may be inconsistent, dates may be insufficiently specified. Ideally, as in this case, there should be access to back-up information which can tease out uncertain details.

> Burke (1992) was interested in the early weeks of admission into care of children in West Lothian. She explored this through analysis of the social work file for each child, drawing up a questionnaire-type format to record the various variables. Several of these features, most notably the reasons for reception into care, required skilful distillation and summary across a range of entries on the case file.

> Currie (1992) wished to identify key perinatal indicators for children at risk of reception into care. Based in a maternity hospital, she was able to access social case histories of 126 antenatal patients referred to the social work department over a three-year period. The records for each case were examined and data relating to a range of primary and secondary indicators extracted. Importantly, Currie highlights the necessity of intelligent use of data from records, and of the importance of seeking clarification where necessary.
>
> > In looking to case material, it became evident early on in the study that to ensure accuracy and minimize error in analysing case paper content, the reading and coding had to be undertaken by the researcher alone. There was found to be a slight variability in the presentation of case material, and where omission of information was present, it had to be supplemented by hospital social work colleagues.

An additional feature of this study was the desire to identify children in the sample who were later received into care. A complication in the cross-matching was the tendency for children to be registered and known by the name of their biological father, even though paternal contact might be absent.

In addition, the study by Ballantyne (1991) reported in Part Three included a retrospective component examining thirty social background reports from each of four area teams. Data relating to a range of variables was extracted in systematic fashion from each of the reports.

Monitoring devices

The need for some form of recording form may arise not just for extracting data from case records but in order to undertake more active monitoring. The classic case-monitoring form was developed by Goldberg and Warburton (1979); subsequent variants loosely modelled on the original can be found in Black *et al.* (1983), Challis and Chesterman (1985), and in studies at SWRC (Fuller and Tulle-Winton, forthcoming). Such forms focus on obtaining a systematic record in relation to a number of cases, data items often including a mix of the objective (demographic variables, services in place, social networks) and the more subjective, for example, an assessment of level of risk. Although they can be used on a single occasion, they are more commonly used when there is an interest in change over time.

Case-monitoring forms require careful design. There very often has to be a trade-off between the desire to gather extensive and complex items of data, and the requirement to produce a form which is both comprehensible and reasonably concise for the individual destined to complete it.

Monitoring devices do not, of course, have to focus necessarily upon individual case monitoring. At its most simple a device could be designed to record the number and type of telephone enquiries received by an agency. Alternatively, there might be a requirement for a form on which could be recorded the interactions between different individuals within some form of residential setting. Observation by its very nature (see below) is likely to generate a requirement for monitoring or recording devices of some form. As important as the clarity of the monitoring device is a mechanism for ensuring its use. There is little point in refining the design of a device if its use is intermittent and sporadic.

Questionnaires and interviews

For some people, the perception of research is that it must necessarily involve some form of interview schedule or questionnaire. While this, it will have been realized, is by no means the case, nonetheless there is a high probability that research pursued by the practitioner will involve one or other of these devices. To clarify the terminology, we use the term 'questionnaire' to signify a set of questions distributed to individuals for self-completion, most generally by ticking predefined categories or writing in answers. An 'interview', by contrast, is conducted face to face or sometimes by telephone. The interviewer will work from some form of interview schedule, although this may range from a very loose set of topic areas to a highly detailed sequence of questions in which use of the exact wording is important.

In theory, there may be situations where both the interview and the questionnaire are equally appropriate; in practice, there are often factors strongly favouring one or other of the devices. Such factors may relate on the one hand to the research question under scrutiny and the nature of the sample that is therefore required, and on the other to the type of information that is sought.

Choose a questionnaire when:	• large numbers are involved • 'facts' rather than opinions are sought • data in a standard format is required • wide geographic coverage is required • time for the respondent to reflect could be useful • long lists of statements need to be read • researcher time is at a premium
Choose an interview when:	• smaller numbers are involved • the enquiry is exploratory • attitudes are sought • complicated reasons for actions are sought • sensitive areas are being explored • complex situations exist • non-verbal responses could be significant • flexibility is required

Questionnaires tend to be indicated when routine information from a number of subjects is required. The questionnaire does not lend itself to the expression of complex opinions and is contraindicated when the aim is to gather in-depth data relating to individual perceptions or experiences. On the other hand, the questionnaire can much more economically gather data for a standard set of variables across a wide range of individuals. The use of particular services, access to particular professionals, or the mapping of social networks may all be more appropriately targeted by the questionnaire. Very often it is the numbers issue that ultimately determines the choice. If responses from a wide range of groups or areas are necessary in order to answer the research questions, practicality will dictate the distribution of a questionnaire. If the interest is not so much in speaking with authority for a sufficiently representative number of people but in exploring in some depth individual experience or response, the interview must prevail.

In practice, it need not be an either/or situation. A broad questionnaire trawl can be followed by in-depth interviews exploring in greater depth emerging issues. Conversely, initial interviews can raise the issues to be pursued in more standard format within the questionnaire.

Design features

Whether an interview or a questionnaire, certain rules must be adhered to in the design of the instrument. Questions must be clear and unambiguous, avoiding terminology that might be interpreted by respondents in different ways, there must only be one question at any one time, the questions must not be biased in any way towards a particular response, and the general complexity and format must be commensurate with the abilities of the respondents.

Whether an interview or a questionnaire, the research instrument must:	• be unbiased • be unambiguous • not lead • use language familiar to respondents • indicate the level of detail required • have a coherent structure, with an introduction and conclusion • not generate unease • be geared in length to the likely tolerance of the respondents

The questionnaire arrives, often unannounced, for the individual to complete. It is therefore essential that both the general instructions and the specific questions leave no doubt as to what is required. There is no opportunity for clarification and the entire purpose of the questionnaire can be invalidated if uncertainty arises around the interpretation of certain of the questions. Thorough piloting of the questionnaire is essential to ensure that these crucial elements, clarity and precision, are in place. In addition, certain principles should be followed in the formulation of questions.

• do not use general terminology – specify the units	X ✓	how long? how often? for how many days, weeks, months …?
• do not use loose phraseology	X ✓	are you better or worse off …? is life better or worse for you …?
• do not ask leading questions	X ✓	why do you prefer being your own care manager? do you prefer being your own care manager?
• do not be one-sided	X ✓	what were the good things about …? what were the good things about …? **and** what were the bad things about …?
• do not ask two questions in one	X ✓	do you think there is a need for short-term/hospice care? do you think there is a need for short-term care? do you think there is a need for hospice care?

It would be the norm for the majority of the items in a questionnaire to be of closed format, whereas in the interview the design will often move towards the inclusion of a greater proportion of open-ended questions. Different question forms are exemplified in Figure 4.1.

The examples in Figures 4.2 to 4.5 demonstrate the translation of these principles into questionnaires used by practitioner–researchers in their individual studies.

The interview, as outlined above, can lie at any point on the continuum from the structured to the unstructured. At one extreme it would resemble a verbal delivery of the questionnaire format (Figure 4.6); at the other the interviewer may be armed with only a loosely formulated checklist of issues to be addressed during the course of an interview (Figure 4.10). Wherever it lies on the continuum in terms of the degree of structure, the

Figure 4.1 Examples of some common types of question.

When formulating questions, it is necessary to bear in mind what the question is for – what issue it will illuminate, what data it will generate, what use can be made of the responses. The following (fictional) examples which might be addressed to a sample of social workers, while clearly not capable of performing identical functions, are all designed to explore some aspect of the *variable* 'social workers' perceptions of intermediate treatment (IT) for offenders'.

Open-ended   What kinds of offence-related problems would lead you to consider an IT referral?

Fixed-choice (1) Which of the following problems would you consider makes a case appropriate for an IT referral. Please tick (you may tick more than one line).

1st offence _____

repeated minor offences _____

truancy and 'bad company'
but not offending _____

serious offence on own _____

serious offence with others _____

Fixed-choice (2) Which of the following problems would you consider makes a case appropriate for an IT referral. Please tick (you may tick more than one line).

1st offence _____

repeated minor offences _____

truancy and 'bad company'
but not offending _____

serious offence on own _____

serious offence with others _____

other (please specify) _____

If you find these categories inadequate, please comment in the space below.

_____

_____

Yes/No

Have you ever made an IT referral after a 1st offence?

Yes/No

If no, go to _____

[Note also: 'Have you made referrals after a first offence?

Often/Sometimes/Rarely/Never]

Agree/disagree

Please indicate whether you agree or disagree with the following statement.

'Referrals to IT should seldom or never be made after a 1st offence.'

strongly   agree   not   disagree   strongly
agree   sure   disagree

Ranking

Please consider the IT referrals you have made in the last year and using the following categories, rank them in order of frequency. Mark 1 against the most common, 2 against the second most common, and so on.

frequency

1st offence_____

repeated minor offences _____

truancy and 'bad company'
but no offending _____

serious offence on own _____

serious offence with others _____

Vignettes

An example of the use of vignettes in this imaginary context would be to construct a short case history (maybe 4–5 sentences) which would illustrate, unambiguously but with sufficient 'realistic' detail, one or more of the categories you are interested in, say a first offender, and ask for the appropriate social work response. The question could be put in any of the above forms.

Figure 4.2 Sample questionnaire: for staff of Waverley residential home for elderly people (after Forsyth, 1991).

When answering, please tick the appropriate box

4 Have you previously worked in any settings listed opposite. If so, please tick the appropriate box or boxes. If not, please go on to next question

Hospital [ ]
Psychiatric hospital [ ]
Other residential [ ]
Home not elderly residential [ ]
Nursing home [ ]

5 Please tick True or False to the following statements

	True	False
Dementia is an illness	[ ]	[ ]
Dementia is caused by a crisis such as the death of a spouse	[ ]	[ ]
Dementia is caused by old age	[ ]	[ ]
Dementia can be caught like an infection	[ ]	[ ]
Memory loss and confusion are always signs of dementia	[ ]	[ ]
Dementia can be cured	[ ]	[ ]

6 Did you have any contact with people suffering from dementia prior to working in Waverley

Yes [ ]
No [ ]

. . .

9 Do you think those people identified as suffering from dementia prior to moving into Waverley should be segregated like this?

Yes [ ]
No [ ]
Don't know [ ]

10 Do you think the residents of Waverley are aware that there is this type of segregation?

Yes [ ]
No [ ]
Don't know [ ]

Figure 4.3   Sample questionnaire: for young children attending a family mediation service (after Lynch, 1993).

I am trying to find out what boys and girls who come to spend time with Tracy think about it. You can help me by filling in this form. You don't have to answer any questions you don't want to.

1   Who's in your Family?
    Circle all the people.

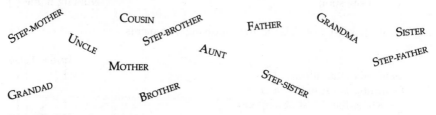

2   Who have you talked to about coming to see Tracy?
    Circle all the people.

Write in anyone I've left out here . . . .

3   Who would you never talk to about coming to see Tracy?
    Circle all the people.

4   What do you enjoy most about being with Tracy?
    Write or draw your answer.

5   When you were on your way to see Tracy for the first time, how did you feel?
    Fill in as many bubbles as you like.

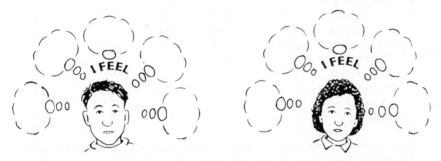

6   When you are with Tracy how do you feel?
    Fill in as many bubbles as you like.

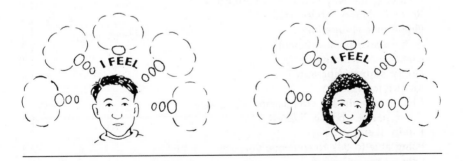

Figure 4.4 Sample questionnaire: for people with eating disorders (after Miller, 1992).

---

6   Who did you first speak to about your eating disorder? (i.e. family, GP, etc.). Please specify _____

_____

_____

7   Which of the following have you had contact with in relation to your eating disorders? How helpful were they?

		Very helpful	Helpful	Slightly unhelpful	Made worse
[ ]	GP	[ ]	[ ]	[ ]	[ ]
[ ]	Hospital doctor	[ ]	[ ]	[ ]	[ ]
[ ]	Friend	[ ]	[ ]	[ ]	[ ]
[ ]	Dietician	[ ]	[ ]	[ ]	[ ]
[ ]	Social worker	[ ]	[ ]	[ ]	[ ]
[ ]	Support group	[ ]	[ ]	[ ]	[ ]
[ ]	Counsellor	[ ]	[ ]	[ ]	[ ]
[ ]	Samaritans	[ ]	[ ]	[ ]	[ ]
[ ]	Occupational therapist	[ ]	[ ]	[ ]	[ ]
[ ]	Health visitor	[ ]	[ ]	[ ]	[ ]
[ ]	Community Psychiatric nurse	[ ]	[ ]	[ ]	[ ]
[ ]	Hospital nurse	[ ]	[ ]	[ ]	[ ]
[ ]	Other – please specify	[ ]	[ ]	[ ]	[ ]

8   What have you found most helpful? If more than one please choose *up to* 3 by prioritizing 1st, 2nd, 3rd in brackets

Exploring why you had/have an eating disorder	[ ]
Changing the way you regard yourself	[ ]
Realistic dietary advice/fact	[ ]
One-to-one counselling	[ ]
Being made to eat differently	[ ]
Confidence building	[ ]
Group support/therapy	[ ]
Medication (drugs)	[ ]
Change in your life circumstances (e.g. new job, partner, house, interest, etc.)	[ ]
Family therapy	[ ]
Being able to talk to someone you trust	[ ]
Other – please specify _____	

Figure 4.5 Sample questionnaire: for parents of children with disabilities (after Hirst, 1991).

4   What sorts of help have you and your child needed since he/she was born? (please tick boxes below)

5   Have you received this help? (please tick boxes as appropriate)

Type of help	Q4 Whether needed		Q5 Whether received	
	Yes	No	Yes	No
Financial	[ ]	[ ]	[ ]	[ ]
Information/advice about the disability	[ ]	[ ]	[ ]	[ ]
Information/advice about available services	[ ]	[ ]	[ ]	[ ]
Housing, including adaptations	[ ]	[ ]	[ ]	[ ]
Aids and equipment	[ ]	[ ]	[ ]	[ ]
Respite breaks/holidays	[ ]	[ ]	[ ]	[ ]
Day care – outwith home	[ ]	[ ]	[ ]	[ ]
Day care – within home	[ ]	[ ]	[ ]	[ ]
Evening/night sitting	[ ]	[ ]	[ ]	[ ]
Personal help/self-care	[ ]	[ ]	[ ]	[ ]
Transport	[ ]	[ ]	[ ]	[ ]
Counselling/support	[ ]	[ ]	[ ]	[ ]
Other, please say what _____				

interview format is obviously much more amenable to clarification or expansion at the time of delivery. This must not, however, lead to any reduction in the clarity of design. The interview situation is a social encounter. Without dominating, the interviewer needs to retain control of the encounter and to ensure that the purpose of the interview is achieved. The researcher must be clear at the design stage as to the boundaries and scope of each question, the degree to which follow-up probes and supplementary questions are required, and the level of detail which should be sought.

Administration

For both the interview and the questionnaire, a major consideration must be maximization of the response rate. The relative importance of such maximization will depend, however, on whether the intent of the

Figure 4.6   Sample interview: for people diagnosed HIV + (after Robertson, 1993).

1   What type of break would be most useful?

		Client	Carer
(i)	day care Monday–Friday	[ ]	[ ]
(ii)	weekly weekend break	[ ]	[ ]
(iii)	monthly	[ ]	[ ]
(iv)	short holiday (up to 7 nights stay)	[ ]	[ ]
(v)	2-week holiday	[ ]	[ ]
(vi)	emergency basis	[ ]	[ ]
(vii)	other	[ ]	[ ]

2   What do you see as being important for the carer during periods of short-term breaks?

		Client Y N N/A	Carer Y N N/A
(i)	time to spend with children	[ ] [ ] [ ]	[ ] [ ] [ ]
(ii)	time to spend with other family members	[ ] [ ] [ ]	[ ] [ ] [ ]
(iii)	leisure time, i.e. reading time alone etc.	[ ] [ ] [ ]	[ ] [ ] [ ]
(iv)	time to catch up with household chores	[ ] [ ] [ ]	[ ] [ ] [ ]
(v)	visiting friends	[ ] [ ] [ ]	[ ] [ ] [ ]
(vi)	socializing, bingo, pub, sports	[ ] [ ] [ ]	[ ] [ ] [ ]
(vii)	work	[ ] [ ] [ ]	[ ] [ ] [ ]
(viii)	support/counselling	[ ] [ ] [ ]	[ ] [ ] [ ]
(ix)	attending own appointments	[ ] [ ] [ ]	[ ] [ ] [ ]
(x)	reassurance that loved one is being cared for (if client, ensuring that carer has personal space, thus care)	[ ] [ ] [ ]	[ ] [ ] [ ]
(xi)	comments	[ ] [ ] [ ]	[ ] [ ] [ ]

investigation is to be exploratory or representative. The more qualitative interview which seeks to explore a range of responses is generally less critically dependent on the participation of the majority of those approached. Questionnaires as a medium, however, are often selected for the very purpose of assembling responses from the range of individuals involved in a particular situation or initiative. If significant numbers from selected groups do not respond, the validity of the interpretations that can be made are limited. Those who did not respond may be from a distinct subgroup whose responses might have been very different.

Despite the strong warnings issued in regard to response rate at the stage when questionnaires were outlined, a substantial number of the practitioner–researchers employed this technique, either on its own or in

Figure 4.7 Sample interview: for residents of Waverley residential home for elderly people (after Forsyth, 1991).

---

4 What was the one thing or person that made you consider coming into Waverley?

5 What happened from then?

6 Did anyone mention that one part of Waverley is different from other parts?

7 Are you aware of any differences?

8 If yes to Question 7, what are the differences that you are aware of?

9 Do you understand what the term 'dementia' means?

10 Have you come across people in Waverley who you think might suffer from dementia?

Figure 4.8 Sample interview: for general practitioners (after Hirst, 1991).

---

7 Do patients ever consult about non-medical problems? Examples. What do you do – e.g. deal with it yourself, or refer on? To whom? (Prompt if not mentioned.) What about emotional stress? What about family relationship problems? What about difficulties connected with physical handicap?

8 Are there any particular problems/situations that you would refer to the social work department? Example.

9 What do you see as the main function of the social work department?

10 In what ways has the social work department been particularly helpful/unhelpful to you and your patients?

11 How could the social work department be more helpful to you/your patients?

12 Do you think you are given enough information about the social work department, its resources, how it is organized, how it functions?

Figure 4.9 Sample interview: for parents of children with a disability (after Hirst, 1991).

3 *Requests for help*
   Did you ask anyone for help at any time?
   Whom did you ask?
   When did you ask?
   What sort of help did you ask for?

4 *Effect of illness/disability*
   How has the illness/disability affected you and your family?
   Could anything have lessened this effect?
   What sort of things?

5 *Suggestions*
   What have you found most helpful in coping with the illness/disability?
   What other things would you find helpful?
   Do you think you have enough information about what is available?
   How could information about resources be improved?
   Whom would you be most likely to go to, if you wanted information or
   help? Why?
   (If social work department not mentioned) Would you consider asking the
   social work department? Why/why not?
   How could the service be improved?

Figure 4.10 Sample interview: for young people attending Millburn Project (after Cornish, 1991).

A When did you first hear about Millburn? Who spoke to you?/What
   information were you given?
   What did you think Millburn would be like? Is it what you expected?

B Why do you think it was suggested you attend Millburn?
   Did you have any difficulties at school? If so, what? e.g. attendance,
   behaviour.
   Have any supports been offered to you at school? e.g. group work,
   placement.
   Have you been excluded from school? How many times? For what
   reasons?
   How is Millburn different from your own school?

C How do you get on at home, with your parent(s), brothers, sisters?
   How do you spend your free time?

D So far, what do you like/dislike about Millburn?
   Has anything changed for you since coming to Millburn?
   What do you hope to gain from being at Millburn?

combination with others. This may well relate to the less time-intensive nature of the data gathering. As stressed above, the design stage for the questionnaire is critical, with obsessive attention to detail required; subsequent administration, however, can be relatively straightforward. Various research wisdom for the maximization of the response rate to a questionnaire can be cited.

To maximize response rate:	<ul><li>explain in a covering letter the purpose of the research</li><li>ask for return by a certain date and be prepared to send reminders</li><li>explain why the respondent has been chosen</li><li>give genuine assurance of confidentiality</li><li>avoid tactless approaches</li><li>arrange the order of questions and the layout so that they make sense to the respondent</li><li>don't start or finish with 'difficult' or sensitive questions</li></ul>

The mistake should not be made, however, of assuming that the questionnaire necessarily has to be delivered by post. Every opportunity to personalize the contact with the individual should be taken. Thus, a social worker might introduce the questionnaire during a visit, explain the background, and leave it to be collected in a sealed envelope on a subsequent visit. Certain situations, for example a drop-in provision, a day centre or a residential setting, may lend themselves to completion of the questionnaire by all respondents at a given time.

The practitioner-researcher often has major advantages in seeking the completion of questionnaires, being able to exploit personal contacts or routes inaccessible to the external researcher. A particularly good example of this is the study conducted by Robertson (1993) to assess the need for short-term and hospice care for individuals who are HIV-positive. A semistructured postal questionnaire was sent to 70 respondents. Those selected to receive a questionnaire were to be those who had experience of symptomatic disease and whose diagnosis fell within the stages III and IV of the WHO classification. Deliberate steps were taken, however, to exclude anyone who had reached end-stage disease or who had been very recently bereaved. This was possible because the population from which the sample was to be selected was known to the researchers. Moreover, because of this contact, the researchers were able to warn of the imminent arrival of the questionnaire. The tone adopted was very much of a partnership benefiting from the knowledge and expertise of the individual, rather than an external body trawling for data.

> We hope you will not object to us having approached you for your views, as we greatly value your experience and insight in this particular area.

In this context, 55 of the 70 questionnaires were returned (24 from HIV-positive individuals and 31 from past and present carers), a remarkably high response rate. The personal contact with individuals allowed the reasons for non-response to be known. Ten of the non-returns were from the HIV-positive group, three being too ill by the time the questionnaire was received, four finding the issue too painful to consider and three not wishing to take part. Only five carers did not respond.

The questionnaire in this case was supplemented by a more informal personal interview to obtain more detailed responses from 15 of the initial respondents. This smaller group of people were selected under the same criterion as the initial group and all who participated did so willingly and with enthusiasm. Whether responding to the first or the second stage, support was available to all respondents both during the study and afterwards.

Other practitioner-research studies reported responses to postal questionnaires more akin to the norm. Garwood (1991), for example, had a 33 per cent response from 144 clients referred for family conciliation by the sheriff court. Garwood was constrained by a factor common to many postal questionnaires, a requirement for anonymity in the distribution method which makes it impractical to send reminders (unless under a blanket approach). In this case, the questionnaires had been mailed directly to clients by the regional family conciliation services. A similar response of 35 per cent (56 of 161) was achieved by Fiona Campbell (1992) who sought the experiences of parents who had used an access centre.

Hirst (1991), interested in the experiences of those with disabilities on getting help, sent out questionnaires through two voluntary organizations. Each organization included its own covering letter of explanation and respondents only gave their names if they were willing to be contacted for a more detailed interview. Of 100 questionnaires sent through an organization for the families of children with special needs, 26 were returned, three without names and addresses. The other organization, a self-help and pressure group, yielded a higher response rate, 58 of 120 (48 per cent), although 18 were anonymous. Certain groups of individuals or particular areas of investigation may yield somewhat higher response rates. In a study of eating disorders, for example, Miller (1992) achieved a response rate of 56 per cent from both workers and sufferers. Both groups had been randomly identified and reminders had not been sent.

Practitioners, as highlighted above, have a natural advantage in pursuing the research interview. Interviews have featured less in the studies of our own practitioners, however, than might have been anticipated on the basis of the general profile of social work research. This may reflect two factors in particular. Firstly, practitioners may have heeded the warning that the face-to-face interview is greedy in terms of time. Secondly, practitioners could often be in the position of having to seek interviews with their own clients or fellow workers. Inevitably, issues arise as to the extent that respondents feel genuinely able to express their opinions. The nature of the study will have an influence. If the focus of the study is on more general features external to the direct involvement between the two individuals there may be no impediment. If, however, the concern is with the direct interaction between the service user and client, a genuine response may be more problematic.

James (1991) examined the matching process in community-based respite care for children with a learning disability. In a project with two workers, it was decided that each worker should interview the other's clients.

> Each interviewer thus had some knowledge of the attempted matches which respondents had experienced, and could for example ask about the carers or service users by name, and ensure that all experiences were included in the interview. It was also possible, however, to avoid too much detailed discussion of situations in which the worker was not directly involved, and encourage respondents to concentrate upon the interview questions.

James discusses in some detail the particular situation of the practitioner interview:

> The interviews largely flowed very well, and respondents often naturally moved on to the next question area during the discussion. The structure of the interview schedule was thus found to be clear and helpful in addressing particular issues, but also allowed for individual comments from respondents. The majority of respondents gave a lot of serious thought to their replies and appeared to be very honest in stating their views. The fact that they knew the interviewer was found to be positive in this, and as she was not their own worker perhaps encouraged them to voice any less positive views or feelings.

Various opportunities may arise for the practitioner–researcher to work in collaboration with colleagues and to enlist complementary skills. As a contribution to the goal of extending research-mindedness this is only to be encouraged. It remains important, nonetheless, that basic principles of good research practice are not contravened; the process of spelling these out can assist in their reinforcement.

Two examples can be highlighted of practitioners using the telephone as an interesting variant of the face-to-face interview. Both were with fellow professionals. Mills (1992) devised a two-part semistructured questionnaire for use over the telephone with social workers referring to Family Link, a volunteer befriending scheme. Part One examined the characteristics of the family referred and the purpose of the referral; Part Two focused on the role of the social worker, other experience of volunteer workers, and their views on the contracting of family support to voluntary agencies. The interview schedule was sent in advance to workers, explaining that the researcher would be in telephone contact in the near future.

> Certainly in terms of time and travel the telephone proved to be a successful medium for gathering data; social workers seem particularly comfortable with this instrument, judging by the inordinate amounts of time they spend on it.

Accessing the social workers was by no means unproblematic however. Fifty-nine workers had made referrals over a two-year period; 50 were still employed in the same office. Several attempts were made to contact each of these workers. Two were off ill for long periods, one was on maternity leave, one was unwilling to participate, two saw no purpose in that a service had not been offered by the agency, and one could not remember the contact and could find no notes on the referral. Of the remaining 43, interviews were finally completed with 30 over a four-month period.

The use of the telephone does not, however, remove the potential conflict between the roles of researcher and practitioner highlighted above.

> The roles of researcher and project worker are potentially incompatible. It is more than possible that social workers *and* families interviewed may not have felt able to adequately express their criticisms of the service offered by both the individual volunteers *and* the scheme as a whole, given that the research role had been taken by one of the project workers of the scheme. Unfortunately, there were no available resources within the agency (either personnel or financial) to provide assistance for the project.

For Kosonen (1992), however, studying family placements in Tayside, a follow-up telephone interview with the relevant worker proved a useful addition to a questionnaire already returned by the same worker. The post of the researcher, Assistant Principal Officer (Fostering) and the perception of the study as a departmental audit, no doubt contributed to maximizing the response rate.

Crawford's study (1992) of the needs of carers of older people illustrates a potential sequence of events to secure a sample of carers for interview. Perth Resource Centre provides day-care services to 120 older people. Older people and their carers were initially contacted by the resource centre manager, a letter briefly explaining the study and asking permission to forward their name and address being sent to each carer. At that stage, two carers indicated that they did not wish to be contacted. From the remaining 118, a random selection of 50 names was drawn and a letter giving a full outline of the study was sent by the researcher. Carers were asked to return a tear-off slip indicating whether or not they wished to take part. Twenty-eight slips were returned, seven of which declined the interview. A potential sample of 21 was therefore secured, with a later cancellation yielding a final sample of 20. Two interviewers were involved in these interviews. The interview schedule was wide ranging and combined structured, semistructured and more open questions. Considerable attention was therefore paid through the pilot stage to ensure that the schedule was applied with a mutual approach and understanding.

A perennial issue with regard to interviewing is whether responses should be tape-recorded. Our own advice to practitioners has been to discourage such recording unless a very strong case can be made. This is not on technical grounds, which often seem to be unnecessarily cited in the literature, but more mundanely on the basis of time constraints. Unless the researcher has guaranteed access to transcription facilities, most importantly the personpower, even a small pile of untouched tapes will deter all but the most dedicated researcher. Although there are several time-saving alternatives to full transcription, merely listening to an hour-long interview demands that hour all over again. Moreover, to listen without making any attempt at a record will barely advance the analysis. If the researcher opts not to transcribe, but to analyse directly from the tape, it has to be questioned whether substantial time could not have been saved by omitting the tape recording and starting the reduction process through full, but inevitably selective, note-taking during the course of the interview. The authors' caution, based on long experience, should not dissuade those who have a strong case for requiring the nuances of debate and inflection that can be secured by the full recording. Increasingly (see below) they may also be seeking transcription for direct input into one of the qualitative data-analysis packages.

Piloting

All instruments designed by the researcher *must* be piloted before they are used in earnest for the main study. Pilot studies have various functions, but the main purpose for the practitioner–researcher is to try out the questionnaire or interview schedule to see if it 'works'. This is an opportunity to check whether the questions and instructions are understood by respondents, whether ambiguities remain in question wording, whether there are unanticipated areas of sensitivity: in general whether the instrument will yield the kinds of data that are sought. It is chastening to discover that, however well the researcher believes the instrument has been drafted, mistakes and room for improvement will almost invariably be revealed. A pilot will also provide valuable information about how long an interview schedule takes to administer or how long a questionnaire to complete, which can be used by the researcher in planning a timetable and in preparing respondents for participation.

Time spent in arranging a pilot study will therefore be well spent. Respondents for a pilot should ideally not be part of the sample for the main study, but should have similar characteristics. This may be easier said than done if there are problems in identifying sample members for the main study, and decisions about who to seek for piloting purposes may have to be adjusted according to circumstances. In general, it is preferable to pilot instruments on less than completely satisfactory samples rather than dispense with a pilot stage altogether. Lessons can even be learnt from trying out a schedule on one or two friends or colleagues if all else fails.

Although these considerations apply most particularly to self-designed instruments, it does no harm to try out in similar ways an instrument borrowed from other studies or a standard scale, to check whether there are any difficulties likely to arise from its application to the particular group that the researcher is planning to study. It is not unusual, for example, for minor changes of wording to be indicated in measures tried and tested on populations drawn from a social or cultural context different to that of its proposed use.

Schedules

The use of standardized assessment schedules tends to provoke strong reactions, some firmly in favour, others equally opposed. We are talking here about schedules developed by those expert in their field to allow standard measurement across a number of dimensions (McDowell and Newell, 1987; Bowling, 1991). Such schedules are subjected to extensive testing in terms of validity (measuring what they purport to measure) and various types of reliability (consistency over time and between different raters).

Scales and schedules can be used either for observation or for interaction (or indeed simultaneously for both). For elderly people, in particular, there are a battery of functional schedules based on observation. Often these relate to activities of daily living and are concerned with summarizing the level of functional dependency of the individual. In the early stages of development, scales focused on basic activities such as bathing, dressing, moving around and eating; subsequently the concept was extended to include activities key to independent living – shopping, cooking, managing money. Examples of such scales in common use include CAPE (Clifton Assessment Procedures for the Elderly), the Barthel activities of daily living index and the RDRS (Rapid Disability Rating Scale). Other schedules, completed with the individual or by a key contact, focus on broader aspects of social and emotional functioning, including morale, life satisfaction and well-being. With regard to the latter, SWRC has promoted the use of the General Well-being Schedule (GWBS) (Hunt, 1992). Scales of this type may be concerned to identify critical levels of distress or may focus on change in individuals over time. Some may target particular groups, for example the well-used Philadelphia Geriatric Center Morale Scale (PGCMS) (Lawton, 1975). Quality of life measures, well represented by Lehman (1983), can perhaps be considered a particular subset of scales of morale and life satisfaction. Other measures, for example the General Health Questionnaire (GHQ) and the Malaise Inventory, may be more directly health related, concerned to identify excessive symptomatology. In certain circumstances, such schedules may be employed as screening devices, ensuring for example that those selected, say for interview, conform to selected criteria.

It may be that the practitioner–researcher, often accustomed to the use of standard schedules and similar tools in the course of assessment, may have fewer qualms about such instruments than some academic researchers. They may be more in tune with the responses of clients and less likely to be unnecessarily squeamish. It is common, for example, for non-practitioner–researchers to express discomfort with schedules which mention suicide or self-harm (Malaise Inventory, GWBS). For the respondent who has experienced such emotions, however, it may be entirely relevant. Particularly in the case of observational schedules, practitioners may often have the skills or the knowledge of the individual necessary for the completion of the scale lacking to the academic researcher.

Guiding principles for the selection of standardized schedules are no different for the practitioner–researcher than for others. Schedules should be appropriate to the cultural context, avoiding for example transatlantic terminology or imagery more readily associated with an alternative care group. Whether for self-completion by the respondent or for use in face-to-face interview or observation, schedules should not be unnecessarily long and should focus clearly on the salient issues. Many schedules, particularly those originating from the psychiatric field, appear excessively lengthy, raising questions of the trade-off between comprehensiveness and user tolerance. Baird and Cook (1991) indeed made a recently developed assessment schedule, the CAFE Form (Common Forms for the Multi-Dimensional Assessment of Frail Elderly by Health and Social Work

Agencies) the focus for their piece of research, exploring the perceptions of the different professionals regarding the form in particular and the assessment process in general.

Select a schedule which:	• scores well on reliability
	• scores well on validity
	• is appropriate to the target group
	• is widely used in other studies
	• does not need specialist training to administer
	• is not excessive in length
	• uses readily understood language

Examples from practitioner–researchers illustrate how such schedules can be employed. Lockerbie (1993), for example, was interested in whether group work could have a positive effect on the behaviour of individuals with dementia. The Individual Behaviour Schedule (Figure 4.11) was therefore used to compare specific behaviours on days with and without groups, while longer-term changes and the subjects' levels of functioning were recorded through CAPE.

Figure 4.11   Sample scale: extract from the Individual Behaviour Schedule.

1 Wandering	
No aimless wandering	2
Occasional and brief periods of wandering	1
Persistent aimless wandering	0

. . .

6 Person	
Almost always responds to name	2
Sometimes responds to name	1
Does not respond to name	0
7 Place	
Almost always knows where she is	2
Sometimes knows where she is	1
Does not know where she is: thinks she is elsewhere	0
8 Time	
Always aware of time (e.g. meals, bedtime)	2
Sometimes aware of time	1
Has no apparent concept of time	0

Franki Campbell (1992) used the GWBS (Figure 4.12), a variant of Dupuy's Psychological General Well-being Schedule, in her study of a project offering community-based support to adults with mental health problems. Although originally designed for self-administration, the lack of reading confidence of some of the respondents led to the schedule being administered by the interviewer. Piloted at an office skills training project, service users 'felt that the questions were tactful and more sensitive than other examples of this type of measure. One respondent noted that the range of responses made it easy to select the most appropriate response in each case'.

The use of schedules is not, of course, confined to service users. Richard (1993), examining relative stress levels in different social work settings used an instrument devised by Warr (1990) which addresses affective well-being, subjective competence and aspiration (Figure 4.13).

Observation

Detailed observation is necessary for the completion of certain of the schedules outlined above, emphasizing the overlapping layers of the methodological repertoire. Observation can be cited more generally,

Figure 4.12 Sample scale: extract from the General Well-being Schedule.

During the past month . . .

3 Have you felt
   depressed?
   - ☐ yes – to the point that I felt like taking my life
   - ☐ yes – to the point that I did not care about anything
   - ☐ yes – very depressed almost every day
   - ☐ yes – quite depressed several times
   - ☐ yes – but depressed now and then
   - ☐ no – never felt depressed at all

4 Have you been
   in firm control of
   your behaviour,
   emotions or
   feelings?
   - ☐ yes, definitely so
   - ☐ yes, for the most part
   - ☐ generally so
   - ☐ not too well
   - ☐ no, and I feel uneasy
   - ☐ no, and I feel very uneasy

5 Have you been
   feeling nervy or
   nervous during
   the last month?
   - ☐ extremely so – to the point where I could not work or take care of things
   - ☐ very much so
   - ☐ quite a bit
   - ☐ some – enough to bother me
   - ☐ a little
   - ☐ not at all

Figure 4.13 Sample scale: extract from a scale measuring job-related and non-job-related mental health (Warr, 1990).

Question	Strongly disagree	Disagree	Neither agree nor disagree	Agree	Strongly agree
Questions about your job					
I find my job quite difficult	[ ]	[ ]	[ ]	[ ]	[ ]
I am not very interested in my job	[ ]	[ ]	[ ]	[ ]	[ ]
In my job I often have trouble coping	[ ]	[ ]	[ ]	[ ]	[ ]
I enjoy doing new things in my job	[ ]	[ ]	[ ]	[ ]	[ ]
My job makes me feel quite exhausted by the end of a work-day	[ ]	[ ]	[ ]	[ ]	[ ]
Questions about your life outside your job					
I feel I am better than most people at tackling difficulties	[ ]	[ ]	[ ]	[ ]	[ ]
I find my non-job life quite difficult	[ ]	[ ]	[ ]	[ ]	[ ]
I make a special effort to keep trying when things seem difficult	[ ]	[ ]	[ ]	[ ]	[ ]
I can deal with just about any problem in my non-job life	[ ]	[ ]	[ ]	[ ]	[ ]
I am not very interested in the world around me	[ ]	[ ]	[ ]	[ ]	[ ]
I sometimes think I am not very competent in my non-job life	[ ]	[ ]	[ ]	[ ]	[ ]

however, as a method of data collection. Methodological texts (see for example Burgess (1984) or Lofland and Lofland (1984)) tend to classify observational activity according to the extent to which the observer takes an active or passive role – participant or non-participant observation. Discussion also revolves around whether those involved in the particular situation are aware of the observational activities ('overt') or whether it is being done without their knowledge. The latter can be termed 'covert' and raises ethical concerns, although common sense would suggest that this should be interpreted according to the context. Observation of the activity levels or verbal interactions between elderly people in residential care should perhaps not provoke the same calls for informed consent as the covert observation of political or pressure groups which may be conducted under the guise of membership.

Whatever the context for observation, some form of recording device is required. This may range from the simplest counting device to a complex analytical tool which starts the move towards converting raw data into categories. Again, such recording devices can vary in their degree of structure, although the context will very often dictate a format sufficiently simple to be used in situations of rapid interaction or movement. Thus, if the frequency or personnel involved in particular interactions is of interest, a chart allowing the various possibilities to be ticked may well be the optimum format. Alternatively, if a more general sense of ethos or style is required, a qualitative account which draws on the observational experience may be preferred.

As with any data-collection technique, a consideration in the selection of the recording technique is the distance being set from the raw data, the extent of transformation. For observational data in its original format there is, of course, the video recording. As with tape-recording of interviews, it should be clear, however, why such a full record is required and the nature of the analysis that is to be pursued.

The practitioner–researcher again has certain advantages in the observational role. The situation is likely to be familiar at least to some extent and therefore preparatory work can be reduced. Moreover, the practitioner may well have opportunities to observe in the context of other duties. These same advantages can also, however, be construed less favourably. The very familiarity of a situation may militate against clarity in the observation, with practitioners being unable to distance themselves sufficiently. Likewise, it is unlikely that an individual well known to the agency could engage in much by the way of arm's length observation.

Mitchell (1993), in his comparison of carer support groups, observed each of his six groups on one or two occasions. His concern was to observe the general style and ethos of the groups, making comment on, for example, the relative roles of carers and professionals, the assumption of the leadership role, the degree of formality and the nature of the content. Such observation allowed him to classify the groups according to the different models of working identified by Twigg and Atkin (1994) and to contrast the perceptions of the different parties. 'Observations of the group suggested that all workers supporting the groups combined models of "co-worker" and "co-client" but with different emphasis.'

Flockhart (1991) observed the first interview between the parties in her study of the perceptions of families and therapists of the changes following family therapy. Nine of the ten interviews were viewed by the researcher through a one-way screen; the remaining interview was video-recorded for later analysis.

Diaries

A range of other, imaginative techniques can be employed. Indeed one of the advantages enjoyed by the practitioner should be the opportunity to capitalize on the variety of therapeutic techniques by extracting the research component. Service users or staff members, for example, can be asked to keep diaries of varying intensities, focusing on specific interests. And these can be in differing formats suited to the particular respondent, including the extended audio recording (or indeed video diary), the written account in free-flow or structured format, or the pictorial representation. In Part Three (Chapter 9), MacVicar describes the use of diaries by staff members to highlight the tasks involved in their role.

Evaluation by rating objectives

A common problem for social work researchers who are studying service effectiveness is that in a sample of users of one particular service, the objectives pursued in individual cases may be highly individualized. No single standard measure is available to assess the success of the intervention. Cornish (1991) addressed this problem, in the pluralistic evaluation referred to in Chapter 3, of the effectiveness of a multidisciplinary project working with children and young people at risk of school exclusion. Following assessment, an individualized set of objectives was identified, with an average of three per case; professionals, parents and the children themselves were each asked after a six-month period to rate the success, on a four-point scale, with which each goal had been pursued. The results were analysed both for individual children and by type of objective, as well as for variation between raters, to show overall success rates and what types of problem attracted the highest effectiveness rating.

Examples of individual objectives within sample	Child A • improve attendance • improve work rate • develop confidence • issues related to home

> Child G
>
> - improve work rate
> - improve social relationships
> - develop strategies for self-control

Making sense of the data

Whatever means may have been used to assemble material, confronting the pile of raw data awaiting analysis is a particularly daunting prospect for the inexperienced practitioner–researcher. Sense has somehow to be made of a mass of completed questionnaires, interview records, observation schedules, rating devices, field notes, or any of the other instruments described in this chapter, together with whatever currently disordered notes accompany them.

For those who have used a quantitative approach, or increasingly those who plan qualitative analysis and can afford the luxury of transcribed interview tapes, the task may be made simpler (though it may not always seem so) by access to a computer, and if necessary to advice on how to use it. Those with such access should have made decisions at a much earlier stage about ways of structuring the data collection to facilitate the transfer of data to a computer file and its subsequent analysis, probably using software such as the Statistical Package for the Social Sciences (SPSS) (Bryman and Cramer, 1994) or for qualitative analysis NUDIST or HYPERQUAL (Tesch, 1990; Dey, 1993). However, many practitioners undertaking research may be without such facilities, and are likely to be analysing data manually. Trying to use a computer without computer skills or expert help reliably available over a period of time is not to be recommended; it can create more problems than it solves.

In fact, the underlying principles are similar whether analysis is by computer or by hand. The process of making sense of the data is a two-stage one. First the data must be checked and 'coded', transformed into an ordered and systematically categorized form. When this has been done, the process of analysis can begin by counting instances and tracing associations between variables.

Coding

The distinction was made earlier between structured and unstructured data. Where data has been collected in a structured form, through, say, a questionnaire with fixed-choice questions, it is already in a partially coded state, and the process of coding is relatively straightforward and mundane. It is a question of assigning a symbol by way of summarizing shorthand, usually a number, to each fixed-choice response. If respondents have been asked to tick a box stating whether they are male or female, most will have ticked one or the other box, though a few may have made no response. The variable 'gender' can then be coded as:

male	1
female	2
no information	3

Where there are partially structured questions, such as those which offer some fixed options but also include an 'other (specify)', the responses to this must first be categorized by the researcher by scanning the raw data, so this additional information can be retained. It may be that three or more separate categories other than those identified by the fixed choices on the questionnaire occur with sufficient frequency to make it worthwhile providing extra codes.

When the data is unstructured, as in an open-ended question, a great deal of work has to be done before coding decisions can be finalized (see below). It is at this point that the researcher realizes the full consequences of earlier decisions about the degree of structure to build into the research instruments.

Analysis

Once the data has been coded by ascribing symbols to categories, it will be possible to produce a record for each case in a sample. If carried out manually such a record may look like this:

case	age	gender	time since referral	etc.
001	3	2	4	
002	1	1	3	

The process of analysis can now begin, first by counting frequencies and then by looking at connections or associations within the data. Frequency counts tell you how many times certain categories appear – how many cases were male or female, how many fell into particular age groups, and so on, according to the coding categories. For those with primarily quantitative data, this will initially produce an extensive array of tables, which the researcher may need in order to properly interrogate the data, but which often contain more detail than is necessary for presentation to audiences or readers. Decisions need to be taken about combining categories and expressing numbers in the form of percentages in order to bring out the information that is most interesting or most relevant to the research questions being addressed.

Table 4.1 Length of stay by outside activity.

Length of stay	No outside activity	Some outside activity	Total
< 3 months	39	32	71
3–9 months	28	42	70
> 9 months	36	78	114
Total	103	152	255

For a primarily descriptive study frequency counts will be of interest in themselves, but analysis is usually more ambitious than this. It seeks not only to answer 'how many?' questions, but also to throw light on how certain variables relate to each other. Are clients with certain characteristics 'more likely' (as statisticians say) to receive certain services? Are certain outcomes associated with particular routes of entry to the system of service provision? Questions of this kind are most simply explored by contingency tables with rows and columns as in the example in Table 4.1, which combines information about how long people have been in supported accommodation units with their participation in outside activities.

A glance at this table would seem to suggest, because of the way the numbers are distributed in each cell of the table, that there is a relationship between length of stay and outside activities. We are not entitled to claim that there is such an association, however, without confirmation by an appropriate statistical test of significance which would tell us whether the apparent disparity of numbers is large enough not to have occurred by chance. Even then, we can only claim that there is an association. It is not necessarily the case that one 'caused' the other. There *may* be a causal relationship, which could be in either direction; it may equally be that each variable is causally related to a third variable not represented in the table. In other words, a number of possible interpretations are possible. The researcher may have reason to favour one or the other if there are other findings which point in similar directions, or if there are theoretical grounds on which the explanation may be plausible.

Particular mention should be made of the inexperienced researcher's approach to statistics. It is, of course, by no means the case that statistical expertise is a necessary feature of research. Respectable and rigorous studies can be carried out with samples too small to be amenable to complex statistical analysis, and logistical constraints on practitioner–researchers will often mean that large samples are beyond their capacity. Sample size does, however, along with heterogeneity in the sample and the ways in which cases were selected, affect the kinds of statements and interpretations that can be offered as findings. If the numbers are large and the researcher hopes to draw firm conclusions about associations between variables, it is essential that expert advice is sought at an early stage in the design of the study, and that consultancy is available during analysis. The statistics most likely to be called upon are those designed to demonstrate whether the differences found in results for different groups are significantly different, i.e. are they likely to be merely chance or do they suggest two distinct groupings? Chi-square and the *t*-test are commonly cited tests of significance. Variants depend on whether parametric statistics are appropriate (where data are normally distributed and are interval or ratio scale, i.e. data intervals are consistent) or whether non-parametric statistics for ordinal (ordered) or nominal (differentiated) data are the requirement. For a clear and comprehensive exposition of these statistics, see Herbert (1990).

Tackling unstructured data

As has been highlighted above, many practitioners relish the opportunity to explore issues of particular interest to them through a series of in-depth interviews. The challenge in such research often occurs at the analysis phase when the breadth and depth of the data, so readily accumulated, can suddenly appear daunting. It is important to bear in mind at this stage that the principle of coding outlined above still holds. The challenge is to reduce the blocks of data present as sentences, paragraphs or other relatively unstructured responses, possibly even as extracts of video recordings, into a manageable number of categories. At the same time it would be a negation of the original recording device if such reduction merely took a highly structured form which excluded much of the detail whose initial attraction had determined the choice of approach.

It can be very easy for the novice researcher to be seduced at this stage by those responses which are colourful and lengthy rather than monosyllabic and mundane. Practitioners must not forget, however, that they are involved in research, not journalism. Equal weight must therefore be given to each of the responses as the analysis process proceeds.

The two stages of coding and analysis are perhaps less distinct for more qualitative data. The requirement is to group the various responses into a number of distinct themes (categories), with the ideal process being characterized by successive refinement. Initial groupings which may have been determined by particular sets of questions may be reformed as overarching, more universal secondary themes emerge.

An analogy commonly used by one of the authors (A.P.) is of a skeleton or tree structure. Attached to the central spine are a number of main ribs or branches, perhaps six or seven in number, to which can be attached most of the pieces of data. These ribs or branches represent the major themes that appear to lie within the data. They are determined through familiarity with the data, through absorption and reflection. Nothing can replace, at this stage, continued immersion in the data. Whereas the coding of quantitative data is a mechanical exercise, to be picked up and put down at will, those who have assembled less structured data must reserve discrete periods of time for the analysis stage. Moreover, the length of time required for this process must not be underestimated. Unstructured data cannot be transformed in a matter of hours and dedicated time must be entered into the research timetable. It is common for professional researchers, no less those who are practitioners, to report astonishment at the time-consuming nature of qualitative analysis.

Some will find it helpful to actually work with a large sheet of paper and to write in references to the pieces of data, ideally in shortened form, at the appropriate points on the skeleton. Working systematically through the various interview schedules or other data-recording devices and allocating the pieces of data to the embryonic themes starts to impose an order and an interpretation on the material. At this stage, it will often be necessary to adjust the boundaries of themes, perhaps to create new ones or to abandon ideas that have led nowhere. The aim is to end with a structure within which the majority of the data sits comfortably. Inevitably, however, there will be some messy bits of data, outliers which will not go readily into the chosen themes. Again, an analogy frequently employed is of trying to close the overfull suitcase: stray pieces of data keep bulging out of the sides. The researcher struggles to contain the rogue elements within the themes already selected or at most to acknowledge a limited number of deviant cases. If the suitcase bursts open too often, however, the set of themes should perhaps be re-examined to make sure that there are not revisions which could lead to a more ready closure.

It can be useful at this stage to seek the cooperation of a colleague or fellow researcher in order to check the reliability of the analysis. In particular, if there is ambiguity or complexity as to the category or categories to which a particular piece of data should be allocated, a second opinion can be sought. Discussion of any differences should clarify the coding schema and reduce any residual ambiguity.

This process of grouping and refinement will hopefully reduce the initial mountain of data to an ordered set of themes. In writing of these themes, the researcher will often wish to invoke the research evidence and to quote from the rich data that may have been collected. Again, however, the warning given above should be heeded; quotation of material should clearly indicate the extent to which it reflects the routine case or the exceptional.

For all researchers, but perhaps most particularly when working with unstructured data, considerable benefit can be gained from early discussion and presentation of emergent findings. The idle query or the request for elaboration can reveal further areas to be explored or, at times, suggest the need for possible revision of initial thoughts. The immersion in the data demanded by the analysis phase can lead also to an obsession with the detail and the particular which obscures more striking generalities. The innocent observation of colleague or critic can often restore a necessary balance and ensure that key issues are clarified before the wider dissemination to which we now move in Chapter 5.

Reporting and disseminating research findings

Publicizing the findings of research is an essential part of the research enterprise rather than an optional extra, yet researchers have not always given it the priority it deserves. There are several reasons for this, ranging from lack of time or energy once the study is completed, through diffidence about the importance of findings, to (even) a misguidedly high-minded reluctance to communicate the rich subtleties of one's conclusions to audiences sometimes impatient for simple messages. These problems in giving proper attention to the dissemination stage apply to all researchers and not all of them are of researchers' making. The responsibilities of both researchers and potential research users for taking dissemination seriously are only beginning to be fully recognized (Richardson et al., 1990; Watt, 1993). Some of the factors at work, however, will weigh particularly for the practitioner–researcher.

Yet the reasons for attaching importance to dissemination should be self-evident. As Whitaker and Archer (1989: 94) remark:

> Research on practice issues, if well planned and conducted, will certainly have implications for practice and, since policy and practice are inextricably linked, for agency policies.

Even if it appears to researchers that the studies they have conducted are purely local in focus, few practice contexts in social work are unique, and practitioners and managers beyond the researcher's immediate colleagues may well profit from knowing about their findings. There is little point in doing research if its results cannot be used to inform debates at the level of practice, management, local policy, in some cases national policy, training or social work theory. And for this to happen, other people must have access to it – preferably in a form which they can readily assimilate.

If one reason for disseminating findings is to inform, and sometimes to persuade, a second derives from the researcher's duty to the clients, colleagues, and managers whose cooperation has been necessary to carry out the study, and whose forbearance may well have been tested during it. As most codes of practice for researchers recognize, participants' direct or indirect contribution to the study creates an ethical obligation to ensure that the research is used. Circumstances may sometimes make it difficult to distribute reports to all participants in a study, if, say, a large anonymized survey has been carried out, and indeed they may not always want this, but they should at least be assured that their contribution will in some form see the light of day.

A third purpose for dissemination is somewhat different. While in some cases the findings of research will be clear and contain readily identifiable lessons for practice or policy, in others the implications may be far from obvious. Findings may appear contradictory, conclusions hard to draw, recommendations for policy problematic. Bringing results to wider audiences affords opportunities for clarifying the significance of uncertain or ambiguous findings and teasing out the practice or policy implications.

Reasons for dissemination	• to inform others of findings
	• to ensure research is used
	• to meet obligations to participants
	• to clarify interpretations and recommendations

This is not to say that the world will necessarily be breathlessly awaiting the researcher's findings. Given the time that will have elapsed since any initial discussions of the study, potential audiences may need to be reminded of its origins and rationale, or even of its existence. The particular interests that others expressed at an early stage may have been displaced in their minds by other priorities. There are, therefore, good reasons for aiming at rapid or interim feedback. Furthermore, findings and recommendations may be challenging to existing practice, to the assumptions on which it is based, or to organizational vested interests. Even if this is not so, 'the facts' rarely speak for themselves, and if the researcher wishes to make an impact at some level, this has to be worked for.

In short, what faces the researcher at this stage in the process is a very particular exercise, or perhaps a series of exercises, in the art of communication – not something (one has to say) always achieved by the conventional research report. The ways in which communicating results may be tackled need to take into account the particular purposes of the undertaking, the receptivity and tolerance of the audience(s), and the time and resources of the researcher. Practitioner–researchers may be particularly daunted by the need to write, perhaps in a style which they assume to require a technical flavour unfamiliar to them. There are, however, different ways of approaching a written report; moreover, much of the culture of social work appears increasingly to be an oral one, and oral presentations have advantages for certain purposes.

Much of what has been said so far applies to all researchers, but the practitioner–researcher's position in his or her agency is likely to involve particular and sensitive issues in reporting results, as well as having some advantages over independently based researchers. In the rest of this chapter, we shall discuss some of the ways and means available to the practitioner–researcher for reporting by both spoken and written word to a variety of audiences. Since no one researcher is likely to use all possible methods, we shall also give some attention to planning a dissemination strategy. And we shall focus on the special challenges involved in discussing critically the practice of colleagues and managers.

Feedback to participants

First, however, we should consider the particular issues involved in feeding back results to those who have in some way participated in the study. Participants include those professionals, clients, or members of the public whose lives or activities have been studied, and those professional managers who have volunteered or consented to agency participation in a study.

The researcher here may have a dual purpose. The first, the clearest example of the ethical obligation referred to above, is simply to give participants an early sight of the research findings, and will often be the first occasion on which the researcher 'goes public'. Indeed, it may be a condition of research access having been granted in the first place that participants are informed of findings at an early stage and have an opportunity to comment before reports are finalized; or the researcher may have offered this in advance as an incentive to take part. There are therefore good pragmatic as well as ethical reasons for giving feedback to participants.

There is, potentially, a second role for such occasions, which may be specifically planned as part of the process of analysis. They are an opportunity for the researcher to check his or her initial interpretation of (especially) qualitative data, a technique known as 'respondent validation' (McKeganey and Bloor, 1981; MacPherson and Williamson, 1992). This can take a variety of forms. Most basically, respondents may be shown a transcript or a summary of an interview ('This is what I understood you to say to me – is it what you really meant?'). While in some cases a respondent's inital off-the-cuff reaction to a question may be the 'valid' one, in others they may have had equally valid second thoughts or be able to pinpoint implicit assumptions not made clear by the context but which are relevant to the researcher's interpretation. More commonly, a section of a draft or interim report may be shown to respondents and comments sought, either in writing or in a group discussion. This is an opportunity for errors of fact to be corrected, and for, if appropriate, a degree of negotiation to take place about the meaning and weight attached to conclusions and interpretations.

Such an exercise is not to be undertaken lightly. It can serve a number of useful analytical and tactical functions: clarifying obscurities in the data; enriching the researcher's understanding; seeking support for findings which at first sight may seem contentious; reminding people that the research may have consequences, and thereby increasing the chances of fruitful impact; alerting the researcher to areas of sensitivity or controversy when wider dissemination takes place. But there are also risks. Wider questions than those studied are likely to be opened up, and disputes may be difficult to control. There may be real or perceived threats contained in the findings. When respondents are the researcher's professional colleagues, it can be particularly difficult to keep the research hat in place. If respondent validation is to take place, it is essential that it be carefully planned, negotiated in advance, and the ground rules agreed, for example that respondents may 'add to the report but cannot subtract unless it is a clear error of fact' (MacPherson and Williamson, 1992) or that disagreements should be recorded.

Feedback to participants in the research is usually easier to arrange with a relatively captive audience of professionals than with service users who may have been interviewed. The reasons for giving feedback apply just as strongly to users, however, and perhaps more so since their voices remain under-represented in research and those unused to being interviewed are particularly vulnerable to misrepresentation. While practicalities may sometimes militate against this, for example because respondents are geographically scattered, it is not impossible to arrange occasions for groups of users to meet, receive early feedback, and be given the opportunity to comment.

Advantages of feedback to participants	• an ethical and pragmatic obligation • respondent validation • immediate impact • clarifying areas of sensitivity

Disadvantages of feedback to participants	• time-consuming • may be hard to stick to an agenda • complicates report-writing

Wider dissemination: purposes and techniques

In one sense, dissemination can start from day one. Telling people about the research from the beginning, keeping them informed of progress, and issuing brief interim reports if the study consists of a number of stages are ways in which potential consumers of the research may be alerted to, or reminded of, its existence and likely significance. In this way, the ground is prepared for the eventual reception of the findings once they are complete. It is when this stage is reached, however, that dissemination begins in earnest.

We now assume that the lonely activity of data collection and analysis is as complete as it is going to be, and that immediate feedback to those who participated in the study has taken place and their comments taken into account. As already stated, the researcher now has a range of choices for the form that wider written or oral dissemination may take. Because time and resources are finite, and because the practitioner–researcher is only too likely to be under pressure to resume normal routines, it is essential that before making these choices researchers are clear about which audience (or more likely audiences) they want to reach, what sort of messages need to be got across, where the impact of the research is to be most fruitfully made.

This is a difficult stage for the inexperienced researcher, who may not feel at all confident of the importance of the work. Nevertheless, it is in the nature of practice-based research, even if only partially successful in meeting its original ambitions, to have real-world implications. These implications, depending on the study, may be for professional practice, for management of services, for the policy that managers and professionals are seeking to implement, for the funding of services, for training, for user groups, for other researchers, or some combination of these.

Potential audiences therefore include a range of constituencies who will have different priorities, expectations of research and degrees of receptivity, and the need to produce different versions of a report is something to which researchers are beginning to become accustomed. The attraction for the researcher of trying to encompass all possible interests in a single document or a single oral presentation must be weighed against the length that this would imply, audience tolerance and the need to target particular constituencies. In general, for instance, the worlds of policy and practice have limited interest in the finer points of research methodology, although (according to their starting points) they may need to be convinced that various stereotypical criticisms of research can be met: that findings, especially from qualitative work, are not 'purely subjective', for example, or that samples are not 'biassed'. For an academic context or for other researchers, on the other hand, methodology, references to the literature and discussion of 'theory' assume a higher profile, and in the special case of a report written as a dissertation for an academic or training qualification the researcher will usually find that certain features are prescribed in the course handbook.

Having said this, and to ease the task, there are generally agreed to be a number of standard ingredients to a written research report.

Written reports

The best point of departure for writing a straightforward report on a study is the original research proposal or plan (see Chapter 3), whose format may conveniently supply most of the main structure. The conventional research report would normally include: a statement of the purpose, background and rationale of the study, backed up by references to both agency context and relevant previous research; a formulation of the precise questions or hypotheses addressed; a description of the methods and sampling strategy (including problems encountered and how they were resolved); an account of the analysis and of main and subsidiary findings; a discussion of conclusions drawn (related back to the original research questions), their implications and any recommendations. There should be a list of references in one of the standard formats, and appendices may include copies of research instruments, and (if appropriate) statistical material not included in the main text.

Clearly, this can be done relatively briefly or at considerable length, depending in part on the nature and scope of the study, in part on the audience to which it is principally aimed, and in part on the time and skills of the researcher. It is important to set aside 'quality time' for writing if this is at all feasible; even so, few practitioner–researchers manage to write reports without some late nights!

There are various guides available for the actual process of writing (e.g. Becker, 1978). The following hints may serve to correct some misconceptions:

- Do not try to ape an 'academic' style if this does not come naturally. Jargon-free language and direct accounts, avoiding for example the passive, will often carry more conviction.
- There is no obligation to report the results of each single questionnaire item, or slavishly to follow the order in which questions are asked when the results are recounted. Presentation in the most interesting manner will often follow a different order, and it is rare for all data which have been collected to be used.
- Similarly, there is no obligation to pack the text with tables, which are often skipped by readers. A few well-presented tables showing the most significant findings, usually in simplified form, make more impact. Other tables can be reproduced in an appendix, or omitted altogether.

- Try to think of imaginative formats, using figures or boxes in the text for example to highlight important points.
- Judicious use of verbatim quotations can make a report 'come alive', though (to reiterate) the temptation to cite only colourful or witty remarks if this misrepresents the predominant tenor of responses is a danger.

Summary reports

Written reports should always include an 'executive summary', not only for readers too busy (or lazy) to read the whole report but also to provide a set of signposts to particular sections of the longer text. The importance of this cannot be overestimated. The need for simple, crisply written summary accounts is repeatedly invoked by policymakers, managers and practitioners who are the potential consumers of research (Sinclair and Jacobs, 1994). Summarizing complex material in such a way that key points are not distorted by simplification is an increasingly important art in the researcher's repertoire, and for the researcher the process of producing a summary is an effective way of concentrating the mind on the essence of what has been found. There should be no embarrassment or false modesty about frankly seeking to grab the attention of those the researcher wishes to reach.

It is useful if the summary is written in such a way that with minimal amendment it can be used independently of the report itself, for wide circulation as a free-standing information or publicity sheet about the study. One format that has been found both useful and popular is a two-page summary under headings such as:

- Title
- Aims
- Questions addressed
- Sample and methods
- Main findings
- Conclusions and implications.

The 'Questions addressed', 'Sample and methods' and 'Main findings' sections may be in the form of bullet points (as shown above), and it should not be assumed that it is necessary or even desirable that both pages should be crammed with closely typed text. The researcher's name and telephone number should be included in case readers are motivated to seek further information. It is of course preferable for this to be produced using a high-quality printer and if necessary taking advice about layout; coloured paper can sometimes increase the visibility of a document in someone's in-tray.

Single- or two-page summaries can be produced in bulk and given wide circulation to people the researcher believes may be interested, which may include colleagues, professional groups and associations, heads of relevant services and agencies, local community or user groups and local media. The summaries need not be on conventional paper – card, bookmarks and even beermats have been suggested as alternatives.

Two rather different approaches to producing summaries, which accompany the longer reports of Macfadyen and Ballantyne in Part Three, are illustrated in the Appendix to this chapter.

Articles for publication

Summary and longer research reports will probably reach a primarily local audience unless large-scale distribution is affordable. Wider publicity for a study, as well as personal kudos for the researcher, can be achieved through publication. Possible outlets for articles on social work research range from scholarly journals such as the *British Journal of Social Work*, through professional journals (like *Adoption and Fostering*) and the more journalistic trade magazines like *Community Care*, to agency newsletters and the popular press. The more substantial of these will have their own conventions for the form and length of articles, which should be obtained and adhered to. Writing papers for academic journals, of perhaps 5000–7000 words, is a daunting and time-consuming task for the inexperienced, and the labour involved must be set against their relatively small readership and (typically) long delays between submission and appearance. Although some academic journals are keen to publish papers by practitioners, and publication in them is an effective way of reaching the academic and training world, it is likely that most practitioner–researchers considering publication will think first of outlets which welcome shorter and less heavyweight pieces.

Oral presentations

Many practitioner–researchers will prefer to present results via the spoken word. Its advantages are the immediacy of oral presentation, with its opportunities for making the account come alive, for answering questions and engaging an audience in discussion. Its disadvantages are the relatively small number reached, and any nervousness experienced by those not used to speaking in public.

If initial feedback to participants has taken place, the researcher will already have had some opportunity to practise oral presentations of the material, and will perhaps have a good idea of which parts of it have to be delivered with particular care – whether in explaining the context of the study, justifying the findings where they may be contentious, or dealing with questions.

Occasions for oral presentation include specially arranged meetings of professional staff, managers or users, conferences, seminars and workshops, and meetings of professional associations or special interest groups. The time allowed for the presentation may range from ten minutes in the crowded agenda of a formal meeting to an hour's plenary at a conference. Another possibility is a training day in which the research is a significant theme.

The researcher should certainly seek at an early stage to arrange meetings of colleagues and/or of senior managers. Depending on the subject matter, this may well be the most tricky of all dissemination events. Audiences may be friendly and eager to hear, but they may also be indifferent, over-expectant, suspicious, or even hostile. Researchers need to make particularly clear in the presentation that they are in the researcher rather than the practitioner role. This is perhaps easier said than done, but the task is eased if it can be established that the methods used have been approved by a professional research consultant and that conclusions reached are firmly grounded in the data. In some respects, however, the insider's position is easier than that of the external researcher because he or she is better informed about agency sensitivities and about the larger agenda on which a study might impinge.

By this time the researcher should be gaining confidence in the material, and be in a position to offer to run a conference workshop or contribute to a training event. Indeed, practitioner–researchers have scarcity value, and may find themselves in demand by conference organizers. Audiences less directly involved in the issues addressed by the study are in some ways less problematic, but the researcher needs to remember that knowledge taken for granted 'at home' may have to be carefully explained to outside groups.

It goes without saying that oral presentations are usually enhanced by visual aids (overhead projections or slides) which should be well produced and legible. Handouts too are useful. Neither, however, should merely repeat the content of the presentation itself.

Poster displays

Poster sessions, a hybrid of written and oral presentations, are often a feature of conferences or other day events. The researcher prepares a poster summarizing the study, and stands beside it while it is on display prepared to answer questions or take part in discussion. The poster may be a version of the summary report which is already produced, but the form lends itself, to those with talent for such things, to more imaginative design featuring graphics or photographs.

Opportunities for dissemination	• research reports
	• summary reports
	• pamphlets
	• items in newsletters
	• articles in social work press or professional journals
	• local/national press
	• academic journals
	• oral presentations (meetings in own agency, conferences, seminars, workshops)
	• poster displays

Planning a dissemination strategy

It would be an energetic researcher indeed – and one with a generous employer – who undertook all or even most of these opportunities for dissemination. And this is without considering such ambitious possibilities as making a video, or more modest ventures like the production of audio tapes which colleagues could listen to in their cars. Researchers therefore need to plan a dissemination strategy, take account of resources and time that can be made available, and decide on priorities. This really involves thinking clearly, once any advance undertakings have been met, about where the main interest of the research lies. There are studies which are of clearest interest to the practitioner's peers, others where the main implications will be for managers, yet others where there are particular lessons for those responsible for training, and so on. It may be hard to decide which are the main audiences, but the choice will influence the kind of occasions targeted for dissemination and, to some extent, the nature of written material produced on the basis of the research.

Since writing different accounts of the same piece of research is extremely time-consuming, ambitions need to be realistic, though access to a wordprocessor makes it easier to produce alternative versions. It may seem heretical to some, but one outcome of the assessment of priorities may be that the conventional 'final report' will not be the most useful way of reporting on a study if its production is not a condition imposed by sponsors or course requirements. Instead of one definitive document, a shorter summary together with a number of papers focusing on different angles produced for different purposes may be preferred. This is another decision which should not be taken lightly. Production of a written report is often the best way for the researcher to make sense of the data, and may be an important motivator for the completion of the study. It also gives the researcher something tangible to show for the effort of carrying out the study. If, however, the amount of time needed to produce it militates against the production of other more useful output, it need not be regarded as sacrosanct.

Practitioners' experience of dissemination

Advice given to researchers to be energetic and diverse in their dissemination activities must be tempered with realism about what is possible, and this will apply particularly to practitioners who may have stolen time to complete a study. The experiences of practitioners taking part in the Stirling programme show some of the difficulties, but also some of the potential. As one of the participants remarked in a follow-up questionnaire:

'There is a real problem about making full use of the research: although it yielded much more than I expected, it has been very difficult to find time to make full use of it ... Dissemination requires energy and determination as well as a conviction that one has something worthwhile to offer.'

All participants who have completed the programme have compiled summary reports, which have been widely circulated in a collection produced by the programme (SWRC, 1993, 1994). These collections attract widespread interest and are clearly an effective way of communicating broad-brush accounts of studies and key findings. Most, in addition, have produced longer reports, these varying in length from a dozen pages to over 140, and a few have, in addition, built the results of their studies into longer discussion papers for internal circulation or discussion by management or (occasionally) committee. The format of the longer reports has also varied, some being fairly standard agency documents while others have had eye-catching glossy covers and content designed for maximum impact. Most participants, too, have made a number of oral presentations in the workplace, most commonly to their immediate colleagues, but also to managers, wider staff groups, and occasionally to management committees. A few only have spoken to groups of clients or carers about their work. Perhaps not surprisingly, close colleagues and (where this was attempted) clients were sometimes found by our participants to be more interested in research findings than their managers:

'Main grade staff were interested in my findings, but many recommendations concerned organization of resources and management, and the managers in these areas did not even attend my talk. I sent them copies and asked for comments but have not received any. I think I should have made it more "punchy" with shorter, sharper conclusions and recommendations. I think if I draft an article and request permission to submit for publication this may concentrate the collective mind of management.'

In part this echoes advice given earlier in this chapter; the additional suggestion made in the last sentence, pointing up the political potency of the written word, is a sound one.

It is a minority who have made presentations outside their immediate work environment. The occasions have included professional interest groups, workshops, training events, and conferences, in one case an international conference. Wider publication of written material has included features in *Community Care*, and one or two longer articles in journals. Editors of magazines and journals are often keen to solicit research conducted by practitioners, and the relatively small number of publications is likely to reflect lack of time and confidence – including confidence in writing – rather than the absence of a market. One participant identified a particular problem in bringing results to a wider audience:

'The dissemination of this study could have been wider had I generalized findings more. This was a very specialized setting and it appeared therefore that the research applied to that setting. I was not good enough, in a couple of general meetings, at making the findings applicable to other settings.'

It will often be the case that practitioner research is based on a circumscribed setting or one that is out of the mainstream; indeed, one of its strengths is to tackle neglected areas. It is not easy, however, for the inexperienced researcher to find the courage to argue for the wider applicability of findings.

Reference has been made to the oral culture which characterizes social work. Our experience would point to the tentative suggestion that practitioners tend to speak better than they write about their research. The liveliness, imagination and enthusiasm with which practitioners present their work to the group at the closing sessions of the course are not always matched by the written versions which follow. Although this points to a strength, it is also regrettable, as it is inevitably through the written word that the widest audiences are reached and, perhaps, that the most subtle or challenging ideas can best be followed through. Professional researchers are themselves not beyond reproach in this respect, but there are lessons here for those concerned with promoting practitioner research. Just as dissemination can start from the very inception of a study, so it does not end when the report is written. Ideally, encouragement and support are needed beyond the end-point of the research.

In Part Three we present some examples of reports written by practitioner–researchers. In a concluding chapter, some further issues of the impact of practitioner research will be discussed.

Appendix

Two examples of reporting and disseminating research findings

Area Team Resource Groups in Strathclyde

Neil Ballantyne
Social Work Department, Strathclyde

Questions addressed

Strathclyde's child care strategy recommends that area teams develop systems and procedures to divert people away from unnecessary involvement in statutory supervision or residential care. Many area teams, but not all, have set up *Area Resource Groups* (ARGs) to fulfil this function. ARGs are meetings of key individuals from within the area team. They meet with social workers who are writing social background reports (SBRs) for the Reporter, and offer advice on appropriate recommendations and on planning a package of resources to meet the needs of each case.

- Are area teams with ARGs more effective than others in diverting children away from unnecessary involvement in statutory care?
- Are those with ARGs more likely to ensure that social workers consider appropriate community-based resources in planning for individual cases?

Methods

Four teams participated in the study, with broadly similar profiles in terms of child population and resources. Teams 1 and 2 had no ARG; Teams 3 and 4 had ARGs. Samples were of children aged 8–18, newly referred on grounds of offending or non-attendance.

- The retrospective study analysed the 30 most recent SBRs from each team.

- The prospective study monitored all new referrals over a four-month period.

Findings

- Diversion. Area teams with ARGs made proportionately fewer recommendations for statutory supervision, and produced fewer statutory outcomes.
- Planning. The ARG teams showed some tendency to make plans in more cases, and to make more multiple plans, though the picture is not consistent between retrospective and prospective studies. The ARG teams made greater use of non-casework plans, especially intermediate treatment (IT) group work.
- *However, this aggregated picture is misleading.* There were significant differences between the individual teams, with Team 1 (non-ARG) behaving in many ways like Teams 3 and 4.

When the data was analysed by individual team:

- Diversion. In the retrospective study, the difference between ARG and non-ARG teams was wholly attributable to Team 2.
- Planning. Although numbers were small, it seemed that both the ARG teams and Team 1 were making plans in the context of an overall lower rate of statutory recommendations, i.e. *they were planning for diversion.*

Implications

The case that ARGs in themselves lead to fewer inappropriate recommendations for statutory care is unproven. Team 1 (non-ARG) diverted many young people from statutory supervision and seemed to be as active in making plans. What accounts for the divergent behaviour of Team 2?

- A difference in population? The study did find that certain factors were associated with a higher risk of receiving a statutory recommendation (e.g. more offences, a previous statutory order, substance abuse), but such variables were not over-represented in Team 2. Just being from Team 2 meant having twice the risk of receiving a statutory recommendation.
- A difference in team organization? This may be part of the explanation. Team 1, unlike any of the other teams, is organized along community social work lines and has patch-based subteams. While it does

not have an ARG, the knowledge that patch teams have of the local area, the close collaboration between team members, and the shared commitment to the principles of community social work may perform the same functions as imposing a specialist ARG on an area team.

The performance of Team 2 suggests that teams can produce different rates of statutory recommendation and outcomes apparently irrespective of the kind and severity of problems experienced by children. It was to try to minimize this that ARGs were developed. The evidence suggests that this may not be the only way to do so, and that other patterns of team organization such as the community social work model may produce similar results.

Preparing or Deterring?: Consumer Feedback on Preparation Groups for Prospective Adoptive Parents

Sue MacFadyen
Barnardo's New Families Project

What I wanted to find out

- What do people need to know about adoption of children with special needs at the beginning stage of the process? How best can this information be shared in the groups?
- The groups are intended to help participants decide whether or not to adopt. In what ways does this happen?
- (A background concern of the study): Can preparation and assessment be combined more effectively?

What the study involved

I contacted people who had attended previous groups. They were divided into two categories:

Category A
  Those who continued and who have a child placed with them.
  Semi-structured interviews conducted with 11 couples.

Category B
Those who withdrew after attending the groups.
19 postal questionnaires sent, 7 completed.

Both categories were asked about their experience of the groups, and the ways in which the groups helped them decide.

What the study revealed

- Attending the groups and hearing about the problems that adoption can bring, is a daunting experience:

  'The groups seem made to kind of put you off.'

- Groups should be informal and relaxed. Participants learned and remembered most from active experiential exercises.
- Experienced adoptive parents should be used more. Their input transforms abstract information into real-life issues. Hearing from those who have already done it gives participants hope.
- People felt they were being sized up or judged by group leaders. This anxiety meant they were not really able to take in what was being discussed:

  'You feel you have to restrain yourself, in case you say the wrong thing.'
  'With hindsight, the groups were helpful, but at the time we weren't really listening.'

- The groups played no part in people's decision to *continue* with adoption. All but one of the 11 couples who proceeded had decided on this beforehand.

  'We could have been put off by the groups but were determined to go ahead.'

- The groups only seemed to help people to decide *not* to go ahead.
- Thus, while not deterring the determined, the groups did not encourage the uncertain.

What the study implies

- Prospective adopters need to know about the realities of adoption. But this information does not have to be presented in ways which feel like a 'test' to participants. Consumers are looking for preparing that is facilitating, that provides time and support to enable them to build on their abilities and test out their strengths.

- This is more likely to happen where the emphasis shifts from 'professional assessment' by social workers to 'self-assessment' by prospective adopters.
- The challenge to adoption workers is to find genuine ways of sharing out this assessment responsibility.

Part Three

Studies carried out by practitioners

The five studies included in this section, examples of research carried out by practitioners from the Stirling programme, have been chosen to represent a range of approaches, settings and subject matter. We also believe that they are sufficiently interesting in themselves to warrant inclusion in a text showing the strengths of practitioner research.

The topics represent something of the variety we have come to expect from practitioner research (see also Appendix 1 for a full listing of topics). Ballantyne's study of diversion from the children's hearings system addresses a set of issues which many other researchers have tackled, but his focus on the particular arrangements made in the statutory authority for which he worked finds something new and important to say. MacFadyen, too, in the well-covered field of adoption placement, examines a particular issue arising in her voluntary agency from the processes by which prospective adopters are prepared for the task. The others, it would be fair to say, deal with subjects less fully studied by mainstream social work researchers. Irvine, based in a community mental health team, reports a study of the social work role with a specific group of clients who have received a diagnosis of personality disorder. Smith, a social worker from a hospital team, looks at the rather special circumstances of social work support offered to parents of children with a serious illness. Another 'minority' social work activity, the provision of respite care for families of children with learning difficulties, is the subject of MacVicar's study.

A spectrum of methodological approaches is on display. Two of the studies (Smith and MacFadyen) based qualitative work primarily on a small number of in-depth interviews with clients – a strategy which we had anticipated would be extensively and effectively used by practitioners but which was by no means the only one. Ballantyne, with a sample which combined retrospective and prospective data collection in order to increase the numbers, extracted data from records and used a pro forma completed by social workers to produce a quantitative analysis comparing different approaches to diversion. The multiple sources of data in MacVicar's study included interviews with both staff and users of the respite care unit he studied, data from records, and staff diaries and observation. Irvine adapted a version of the case review form to record basic data about a sample of clients and combined that with staff interviews.

It is worth noting that three of the researchers were directly involved in the activities they were studying, Smith in particular discussing the task of interviewing her own clients (which turned out not to be as problematic as expected), whereas MacVicar and Ballantyne were at one remove. The agency context also reflects the range represented in the programme, with three participants from the statutory sector and two from voluntary agencies.

The studies are reported by the practitioners themselves in their own distinctive styles, with minimal editing to ensure a degree of consistency of presentation; references (unlike the rest of the book) follow at the end of each chapter. In one case (MacVicar) the report has been abridged.

Chapter 6

Diversion at the point of entry to the Scottish children's hearings system: area team resource groups

Neil Ballantyne
Formerly Strathclyde Social Work Department

Introduction

Diversion

The term 'diversion' has been used to describe a range of policies and practices at several different levels of intervention. Tutt and Giller (1984a) suggest that we can characterize three broad types of diversionary scheme: diversion from crime, through the use of initiatives like social education or youth activity programmes; diversion from court or official processing, by selective non-intervention or the police cautioning of first-time offenders; and diversion from custody or care, through the provision of carefully targeted alternatives to care or custody. This study is concerned with the second of these forms of diversion, diversion from official processing, in the context of the Scottish system of juvenile justice – the children's hearings system.

The Scottish children's hearings system

The Scottish children's hearings system, established in response to the Kilbrandon Committee report of 1964 and framed in the legislation of Social Work (Scotland) Act 1968, is one of the most thoroughly welfarist models of juvenile justice in the world. Notions of crime and punishment are not part of the official vocabulary of the children's hearings system or its agents and, most importantly for our present purposes, the system does not formally differentiate between children and young people who commit an offence, truant from school, or are in need of 'care and protection'. However, the hearings system has, in its procedures and practices, a large capacity to divert young people away from formal processing.

The gates to the children's hearings system are kept by an official known as the Reporter who receives all referrals to the system and determines, firstly, whether there is sufficient evidence to proceed and, secondly, if the child or young person is in need of compulsory measures of care. The reporter exercises considerable discretion in making this latter decision, and is assisted in so doing by the local authority social work department. The social work department have a statutory obligation to prepare for the reporter a social background report (SBR) on the child or young person. The social worker writing the SBR assesses the need for compulsory measures of care, and makes a recommendation as to the most appropriate course of action. Therefore, within the children's hearings system, the social worker's SBR is a key document influencing the decision of the reporter and, if compulsory measures of care may be necessary, influencing the disposal of the children's hearing. The available evidence suggests a high correspondence between the recommendations of social workers and the decisions of reporters and children's hearings (Martin *et al.*, 1981; Lockyer, 1988).

If compulsory measures of care are not deemed necessary, then the reporter may take 'no formal action', refer to the police or juvenile liaison officer for a police warning, or refer to the social work department for voluntary advice and assistance (Section 39(2) of the Social Work (Scotland) Act (1968)). The most frequent course of action taken by the reporter, on all grounds of referral, is to take 'no formal action'. The proportion of 'no formal action' decisions has been steadily rising from 38 per cent of all cases in 1981 to 53 per cent of all cases in 1991. This discretion is exercised most in referrals on offence grounds – of all offence ground referrals in 1991, only 31 per cent were referred to a children's hearing (Scottish Office, 1993).

Systems management in the Scottish context: ambivalence and ambiguity?

In England and Wales, arguments for the diversion of young people in trouble from the juvenile justice system have been associated with a critique of the unintended consequences of the Children and Young Person's Act 1969. The CYPA was intended to result in a less frequent use of care and custody for young people in trouble, but actually led to a dramatic increase in both measures during the 1970s. Responsibility for this outcome was attributed by many commentators to the introduction of welfare considerations in a juvenile justice context (Morris *et al.*, 1980) and, in particular, to the content of social enquiry reports prepared by social workers for the juvenile courts. Research findings suggested that social enquiry reports, which focused on the welfare needs of young offenders, tended to result in a greater use of intrusive measures – like care orders or custodial sentences – for relatively trivial offences (Thorpe *et al.*, 1980). The 'Justice for Children' lobby led an assault on the application of welfare principles in a natural justice context and on the discretionary powers of social workers (Morris *et al.*, 1980). They argued for a juvenile justice system that was based on 'just deserts', or punishment in proportion to the offence committed, that emphasized the role of due process and children's rights and advocated the application of the principles of systems management including diversionary procedures.

The 'welfare' versus 'justice' debate that raged in England and Wales during the 1980s had little impact on child care practice in Scotland. The more radical proposals of the Kilbrandon Report, and the virtual abolition of custody for all but the most serious offenders under 16 years of age, made talk of 'just deserts' seem misplaced and eccentric. Nonetheless, as research findings on the more negative aspects of residential provision within the child care system continued to mount (DHSS, 1985), attention was concentrated in Scotland on the application of systems ideas – such as 'gatekeeping', 'monitoring' and 'diversion' – to the problem of managing entry into residential provision. Indeed, during the mid-1980s these concepts influenced the thinking of intermediate treatment (IT) workers, social workers and strategic planners. They impacted on youth and child care policies developed by many Scottish local authorities and, arguably, were partly responsible for the steady decline in the use of residential child care in Scotland (ITRC, 1986).

However, the application of systems ideas in the context of a welfare-based system of juvenile justice, contains some 'conceptual ambiguity' (Morris and McIsaac, 1978) that has a resonance with the 'welfare' versus 'justice' debate. This ambiguity and ambivalence towards the application of systems ideas in a welfare-based system of juvenile justice can be detected throughout 'The Report of the Inquiry into Child Care Policies in Fife' (Kearney, 1992). The problem arises, in part, because of the children's hearings system's single route for processing young people who offend, truant, or are in need of 'care and protection'. Raynor (1993) – commenting on the English and Welsh child care system – cautions against assuming that systems thinking, successfully applied in a juvenile justice context, can be applied in quite the same way within the broader field of child welfare (Raynor, 1993: 7):

A further important difference between the juvenile justice system and the broader child welfare field is that in the former, welfare will often be promoted by doing less to a child (e.g. diversion, decarceration) whereas in the latter, there may be a clear duty to intervene positively.

In the Scottish context, the use of systems management to divert children and young people from welfare interventions can seem to run the risk of failing to identify or meet welfare needs. This ambiguity has led to widely divergent interpretations of where and when it is appropriate to divert, and to differing perspectives on the application of the principle of 'minimum necessary intervention' (Kearney, 1992).

In Scotland, the term 'minimum necessary intervention' is in more common usage than the term 'diversion' (at least in relation to children and young people within the children's hearing system). At the level of entry to the system, it is often defined as the use of voluntary measures in preference to statutory measures, rather than non-intervention. This preference for the use of voluntary measures is echoed in Scottish Office guidelines for the use of home supervision requirements (SWSG, 1987):

> A guiding principle for local authorities must be to offer children and their families help, support, and guidance at an early stage, and by this means prevent the need for more formal or compulsory measures.

The Strathclyde care strategy

In 1985, the social work department of Strathclyde Regional Council published a child care policy document entitled 'A Care Strategy for Young People in Trouble'. The care strategy was a formal statement of the department's commitment to working with young people in trouble in the community and it espoused several key principles two of which were: 'to have the minimum intervention necessary to effect a process of change'; and 'to devise strict criteria and procedures to ensure that all possible voluntary resources are used before statutory measures are considered'.

The report also stated that area teams, as the first point of contact, had a crucial role to play in developing the strategy and that one way of so doing was to establish procedures to:

> ensure that all community and voluntary resources are used wherever possible to prevent further 'official processing'.

Area Resource Groups

In order to progress the objective of diversion from initial processing some area teams in Strathclyde region established Area Resource Groups (ARGs) to screen recommendations and assist planning in social background reports (SBRs) prepared for the reporter. ARGs consist of meetings of key individuals from within the area team including, normally, a senior social worker, a senior IT worker and a social worker or IT worker. Where a social worker, writing a social background report for the reporter, is considering a recommendation other than no further action, they attend the ARG prior to the submission of the report. The ARG then agrees the appropriate SBR recommendation and, where required, a package of resources to meet the needs of each individual case.

This study explores the decisions and outcomes of teams with and without ARGs and questions the effectiveness of ARGs in relation to two of their aims:

- Are area teams that operate ARGs more effective than other area teams at diverting children and young people away from unnecessary involvement in the statutory care system?
- Are teams with ARGs better at ensuring that social workers consider appropriate community-based resources in planning for individual cases?

Methodology

The area teams

Four area teams participated in the study, two of which operated ARGs and two did not. Teams A and B were teams which did not operate an ARG and whose recommendations and plans were based on the individual decision of social workers in consultation with their senior. Teams C and D were teams where ARGs operated as described above.

The four area teams had differing populations but had access to a similar range of child care resources including community-based IT within the team, and more intensive IT provisions in the wider district. Non-ARG teams A and B were both part of the same district and had adjacent geographical boundaries. The study did not control for team organizational structure; however, as discussed below, this may have had an influence on the findings: non-ARG team A was described by the team manager as a community social work team whilst the other three teams operated a generic model of team organization.

The referrals

The study focused on the recommendations and plans of social workers in relation to referrals for social background reports from the reporter to the children's hearing. The sample excluded 'care and protection' cases and included only those aged 8 to 16 who were new referrals from the reporter (i.e. there was no *current* involvement with the case in either a voluntary or statutory sense), and who were referred on grounds of offending or non-attendance at school.

The research design

There were two aspects to the research design: a retrospective study and a prospective study. The retrospective study consisted of a content analysis of 30 SBRs from each area team. The SBRs were analysed to determine the characteristics of the child referred (e.g. age, sex, grounds of referral, offence type, offence number); the social worker's assessment of problem areas (e.g. family, school, peer group, substance abuse, child abuse); planned interventions in relation to the case (e.g. individual work, family work, school liaison work, IT group work); and the social worker's recommendation. In addition, information was obtained on whether or not the case was discussed at an ARG and on the recommendation made by the ARG. The retrospective study included analysis of the actual outcomes, i.e. the decision of the reporter and/or the disposal of the children's hearing.

The prospective study monitored social workers' assessments, plans and recommendations using a self-completion pro forma to gather information on all relevant referrals from each team over a four-month period. The pro forma also asked social workers to assess the severity of problems identified (e.g. high, medium or low). Due to the timescale of the research – and the time lapse between SBR recommendation and reporter's or hearing decision – it was not possible to monitor the outcomes of the prospective SBR recommendations. There were 120 cases in the retrospective study and an additional 81 in the prospective study giving 201 cases in all.

The two studies are combined for analysis on variables where such a combination can be made, but there are problems in so doing. It is possible that, in the prospective study, the social workers' planning or assessment may have been influenced by the range of options presented in the pro forma. It is also possible that the research monitoring of social workers' recommendations may have influenced these recommendations in some way: the potential effect of monitoring on practice is, after all, part of the rationale for the establishment of ARGs. The findings of the retrospective study, therefore, which analysed decisions and plans made prior to the start of the research, may be a more reliable indication of typical practice in each of the teams.

Findings

The small sample size, especially in relation to the proportion of cases where compulsory home supervision (S.44(1)(a) SWSA) was recommended,

Table 6.1 Combined studies – social workers' recommendations.

Social workers' recommendations	Non-ARG teams		ARG teams		
	Team A	Team B	Team C	Team D	Totals
Home supervision: S.44(1)(a)	6	15	3	4	28
Voluntary measures: S.39(2)	6	6	1	10	23
No further action	33	33	36	26	128
Other	4	4	4	10	22
Totals	49	58	44	50	201

make firm conclusions hazardous. Nonetheless, the findings – in relation to the pattern of recommendations and outcomes in particular – are interesting and require explanation.

SBR recommendations

This section presents findings of the recommendations made by social workers to the Reporter and/or children's hearing. The recommendations from both studies are presented in a combined table (Table 6.1).

When recommendations from non-ARG teams A and B are combined and compared with the pattern of recommendations of the ARG teams C and D we find a statistically significant difference ($p < 0.05$) in the pattern of recommendations. One source of this difference is undoubtedly the differential use of the recommendation for compulsory home supervision. A recommendation for home supervision was made in 19.6 per cent of the combined non-ARG team cases, and in only 7.4 per cent of the ARG team cases. However, Table 6.1 reveals a more complex pattern of recommendations than this finding suggests. The greater use of the compulsory supervision recommendation made by the non-ARG teams is wholly attributable to social workers in team B who make this recommendation in over one-quarter of all cases.

There is also a striking difference, though not statistically significant, between the results of the two studies. The prospective study found an overall lower proportion of statutory supervision recommendations, a higher proportion of no further action recommendations in all teams except team C (which was already very high) and a reduction in 'other' recommendations. These differences, and others described below, suggest an effect of the research monitoring process on social workers' decision-making.

Table 6.2   Referral outcomes – retrospective study.

	Non-ARG teams		ARG teams		
Referral outcomes	*Team A*	*Team B*	*Team C*	*Team D*	*Totals*
Residential supervision: 44.1(b)	0	0	0	1	1
Home supervision: S.44(1)(a)	3	17	7	6	33
Discharged	2	3	4	2	11
Voluntary measures: 39(2)	5	2	2	7	16
No further action	20	8	17	14	59
Totals	30	30	30	30	120

The role of the ARG

It is usual practice that social workers discuss all case referrals at an ARG, unless the intention is to recommend 'no further action' and this recommendation is considered likely to be accepted. In the retrospective study, half of the team C social workers did not discuss their cases at an ARG. In all but one of these cases, however, the recommendation was for 'no further action'. In the team C cases where the social worker did attend an ARG, 67 per cent of the recommendations were for no further action, 20 per cent for voluntary measures and 13 per cent for a statutory home supervision requirement. In this team the vast majority of ARG recommendations corresponded with the SBR recommendation.

In team D, the retrospective study found that three-quarters of cases were discussed at an ARG, but over half of the actual SBR recommendations did not correspond with the recommendation made by the ARG. In addition, of the ten cases not discussed at an ARG, three of the recommendations were for statutory supervision and one for voluntary measures. Overall, the ARG seems to have had very little influence on SBR recommendations made by social workers in team D and, consequently, its performance may not really reflect the potential influence of an ARG.

Once again, there was a striking difference between the retrospective and the prospective studies suggesting an influence of the research monitoring. In the prospective study, team C was found to have a perfect correspondence between ARG recommendation and proposed recommendation and in team D there was an almost perfect correspondence.

Referral outcomes

The retrospective study (Table 6.2) monitored the actual outcomes of the referrals in terms of the action of the Reporter and, where a hearing was convened, of the children's panel. The most striking finding is the

Table 6.3 'Other' recommendations by outcome – retrospective study.

Outcome	No recomm-endation	Children's hearing	Residential assessment	Continue hearing	Totals
Home supervision:					
S.44(1)(a)	1	6	1	–	8
Discharged	–	2	–	–	2
Voluntary measure:					
39(2)	1	–	–	1	2
No further action	4	1	1	–	6
Totals	6	9	2	1	18

difference in outcomes between the two non-ARG teams: team A has the lowest proportion of statutory outcomes of all four teams and team B has the highest proportion – over half of the referrals entering statutory supervision. It is notable that team A also has the highest degree of correspondence between the recommendations of social workers in SBRs, and subsequent decisions by the reporter and children's hearing (a correspondence rate of 80 per cent).

In ARG, team C (the team where ARG decision-making does seem to have an influence over SBR recommendations), despite making by far the lowest proportion of statutory recommendations, the children's hearing placed two-thirds more young people on compulsory supervision orders than were recommended by the social worker's SBR.

'Other' recommendations

In 26 cases in the combined studies an 'Other' type of recommendation was made. Although the number of 'Other' recommendations is small we can see from a presentation of the findings (Table 6.3) of the retrospective study, that the outcomes in terms of entry to compulsory supervision are striking.

Of particular interest are the number of recommendations made that a child or young person 'appear at a children's hearing'. From an analysis of all of the reports containing this recommendation, it is clear that the social workers did not consider that compulsory measures of care were necessary, but believed that there may be some cautionary effect to be gained from an appearance at a hearing. The explanation that social workers gave for these recommendations usually included statements like to give the child a 'warning' or to 'emphasize the seriousness' of the situation. The cases involved were mostly offence grounds only. Two-thirds of these recommendations resulted in a compulsory home super-vision requirement: two of the 'appear at a children's hearing' recom-mendations were from non-ARG team A; four from non-ARG team B; and three from ARG team C.

Type and number of plans made

In the retrospective study, the overwhelming majority of interventions, not surprisingly, were planned in relation to cases where the recommen-dation was for voluntary measures or statutory home supervision. Planned interventions were proposed in over one-third of all cases. The number of plans made varied between one and three, and the two ARG teams produced SBRs with three plans twice as often as the other two teams.

The majority of plans in all teams are for individual and family case-work, though ARG team C made a larger proportion of plans for school liaison and both of the ARG teams make proportionally greater use of IT group work.

In the prospective study, over one-third of all cases have interventions planned and the proportion of cases with three plans increases in non-ARG Teams A and B. This latter finding may be a further example of an effect of the research monitoring exercise.

The sample

It is possible that the differences that emerge between teams are wholly explained by differences in the characteristics of the sample. The sample was homogeneous to the extent that all referrals were cases in which there was no current involvement, and all were on the grounds of an offence or non-attendance at school. There were, however, differences in other characteristics of each case, and in the social worker's assessment of the number and type of problems. Moreover, some of these differences in characteristics and assessed problems have been associated in this study, and in other studies (Martin *et al.*, 1981), with differences in SBR recommendation and in outcome.

Characteristics of the sample

On the characteristics of age, grounds of referral, offence type and number of offences committed, the sample as a whole – including the retrospec-tive and prospective cases – was very similar to the characteristics of the population of children and young people referred to the reporter on offence and/or truancy grounds across Scotland in the year of the study (Scottish Office, 1993).

An analysis of the characteristics of age, sex, grounds of referral, number of grounds of referral, type of offence and number of offences found relationships between some of these variables and recommendations similar to those identified by Martin *et al.* (1981), but could find no systematic or significant difference between team samples that might explain differences in the team patterns of recommendations or outcomes.

Social workers' assessment

It was also possible to establish a relationship between cases with certain types or combinations of identified problem, the number of problems identified, the severity of problems and the likelihood of a recommendation for statutory supervision. However, it was not possible to explain the SBR recommendations with reference to these factors alone. Although different teams had different patterns of assessed problems they were not systematically related to the pattern of recommendations. For example, in almost half of the cases where school non-attendance was identified by social workers as a problem there is a recommendation for statutory home supervision and in over half of the cases where substance abuse was identified there is a statutory recommendation. However, there is no relationship apparent between the identification of such problems and the different patterns of team recommendations. Although non-ARG team A and non-ARG team B differ markedly in SBR recommendations and outcomes, they had a closely similar profile of the type of problems identified by social workers.

Discussion

There is some support, in the retrospective study, for the view that when interventions are required, teams with ARGs plan more interventions and make more use of IT as a community-based resource; ARG teams also make consistently fewer recommendations for compulsory home supervision. But there are differences between the two ARG teams and the two non-ARG teams that require further discussion.

The ARG teams

In team C, the ARG was attended by social workers when appropriate – that is, in all cases other than those where a 'no further action' recommendation was clearly indicated – and almost all ARG recommendations were translated into SBR recommendations.

By contrast, in team D, the retrospective study found that social workers did not implement the ARG recommendation in half of all cases discussed – often submitting reports with no recommendation and sometimes avoiding going to the ARG at all. This finding suggests that procedures to attend the ARG, and to follow through with its decision, were either not known to team D social workers or were being subverted. This finding changed markedly in the prospective study where – perhaps as a result of the research monitoring exercise – there was a near perfect correspondence between ARG recommendation and proposed SBR recommendation in team D.

Clearly, if ARGs are to be given an opportunity to demonstrate effectiveness then social workers require to attend and to follow through recommendations. But part of the problem may be a perceived imposition of the ARG on social workers who are unconvinced of its value. In this kind of context the ARG may be seen as an essentially 'mechanistic' screening device which threatens to undermine the autonomy and professional integrity of social workers. These remarks are speculative but reflect issues arising from discussions on the use of ARGs with fieldworkers.

Both ARG teams make consistently less frequent use of the recommendation for compulsory home supervision than the non-ARG teams, team C making the least frequent use of this recommendation. However, team C also had the strongest divergence between the social worker's SBR recommendation and the decision of the children's hearing to require a home supervision order: less than one-third of the hearing decisions for compulsory home supervision were supported by the SBR recommendation. This is a problematic issue for 'minimum necessary intervention' and is discussed further below.

Both team C and team D made proportionally more plans than either of the non-ARG teams, and planned to use IT group work in almost half of all cases where plans were made. The simple fact of the involvement of IT staff in the ARGs may well account for the greater tendency of the ARG teams to make proportionally more use of IT as a resource.

The non-ARG teams

One of the most striking features of the whole study is the widely divergent recommendations and outcomes between the two non-ARG teams; all the more so because the two teams are located in the same social work district, share the same reporter and pool of children's panel members, and had referrals with a very similar profile of case characteristics and assessed problems.

Team A's use of the recommendation for compulsory measures is slightly higher than the ARG teams in the prospective study, but very similar in the retrospective study. It achieves the lowest proportion of children entering the system with only 17 per cent referred on to a hearing, and only one in ten entering compulsory supervision. Team A also had the highest correspondence between SBR recommendations and the actual outcome (80 per cent) suggesting that the reporter and children's hearings have a high degree of confidence in the recommendations of this team.

This picture contrasts sharply with neighbouring team B where social workers make the greatest use of a recommendation for compulsory home supervision, doing so in one-third of cases in the retrospective study. This proportion falls in the prospective study, but the trend is still to make greater use than other teams. In the retrospective study team B made almost half of the 'Other' recommendations that the child attend a children's hearing, all of which resulted in compulsory supervision requirements. Overall, two-thirds of referrals to team B in the retrospective study were referred on to a hearing, and over half of all referrals entered compulsory supervision.

Implications for practice

The issues arising from the writing of reports for a juvenile justice system can be considered at three different levels of analysis (Tutt and Giller, 1984b; Bottoms and Stelman, 1988): the *individual report writer's practice*; the *organizational context* of the report writer's agency – which includes issues such as 'monitoring' and 'gatekeeping' of reports and their recommendations; and finally, the *systems context*, or the relationship between the report writer's agency and other parts of the local juvenile justice system. The three levels of analysis are not entirely discrete, and issues and action at one level will influence issues and action at each of the others. This study was focused on the effect of ARGs, and therefore at the organizational level, but there are issues arising from the study with implications for practice at each of the other levels.

Level one: individual practice
The small number of SBRs with a recommendation of 'attendance at a children's hearing' was of concern. Two out of every three of these recommendations entered compulsory supervision. There may, of course, have been other reasons for the outcomes described, but in none of these cases did the social worker involved identify a need for compulsory measures of care. Given the findings of Martin *et al.* (1981) about the perceived stigma of hearing attendance, and the negative reaction of children and young people to a 'threatening and exhorting style' of communication from panel members, it is hard to see in what way this type of recommendation might be in the child's 'best interests'. Most recommendations for an 'appearance at children's hearing' were on offence grounds and, perhaps, a recommendation to the reporter to refer back to the police for a warning would have been more in keeping with the

social worker's intentions, and with the principle of 'minimum necessary intervention'.

Level two: the organizational context
The apparently unaccountable divergence between the two non-ARG teams is suggestive of territorial injustice, if we can use such a term in a welfare context. Both from the findings, and from the researcher's subjective impressions on reading the reports, it would appear that many of the referrals made to team B would have received a less intervention-ist recommendation if they had been referred to team A just a few miles away. This wide divergence in outcomes between different areas was part of the rationale for ARGs and may be taken as support for the principle of ARGs. But, why is it the case that team A has the lowest overall proportion of statutory outcomes in the retrospective study, the highest overall correspondence between SBR recommendations and ac-tual outcomes, and does not operate an ARG? Is this a chance result, or is there anything about the organization of team A that might explain this finding? Perhaps the fact that team A is described as a community social work team may hold part of the explanation. Although the team does not operate an ARG to screen recommendations, the team manager has a high commitment to information management systems and does retrospectively monitor SBR report recommendations and outcomes. Also, in another context, Fuller and Petch (1991) have remarked on the differ-ential outcomes between community social work teams and other forms of team organization in social work: they suggest that some of the activ-ities of the community social work team in their study 'might be charac-terized as preventive rather than case finding' (Fuller and Petch, 1991: 483).

The use of ARGs, as a method of organizational control of decision-making, is an essentially 'mechanistic' approach (Burns and Stalker, 1966) and as such may be susceptible to subversion by the more informal proc-esses of the social work team (this may be part of the explanation for the subversion of the ARG decisions in team D); the importance of informal team influences on planning and decision-making in child care has been noted by Vernon and Fruin (1986). It may be possible to develop control systems that recognize and utilize the influence of informal processes, and focus on the development of shared values and 'team culture', to assure the desired outcome. Clive Miller, in a report on the decentraliza-tion of social services for the Social Services Inspectorate (Social Services Inspectorate, 1988) has argued that decentralized organizations, such as community social work teams, may adopt a different organizational style and that control may be managed by 'organizational culture' rather than structure. He refers to Peters and Waterman's (1982) work on successful American business corporations to support this innovative approach to organizational style where 'Delegation and autonomy coordinated by teamwork rather than structures and procedures are the order of the day'.

It is at least possible that members of team A are responding to a 'team culture' that values 'minimum necessary intervention', and that 'team culture' or norms are able to influence practice as much as, or more than, an administrative screening mechanism. It is equally possible that members of team B are responding to a 'team culture' of a different kind, which encourages a much lower threshold for the consideration of compulsory measures of care. These remarks are, of course, wholly speculative. However, this notion of 'team culture' or ethos, and of the informal influences on social work decision-making, is a very interesting one, and worthy of more detailed exploration in future research.

Level three: the systems context
Diversionary recommendations are of little use unless they influence the proportion of diversionary outcomes, and part of the role of ARGs in area teams is to promote such diversion. A glimpse of the relationship between different parts of the local system in different areas is offered by the correspondence between the decisions of reporters and children's hearings, and the recommendations of social workers.

Team C is the team where the ARG seems to make most impact, and this team makes the least use of recommendations for compulsory home supervision. However, of all of the children and young people who enter home supervision from this team, less than one-third did so on the recommendation of a social worker. If this represented a trend then it is a problematic one. ARGs can influence SBR recommendations but cannot effect change unless the recommendation is credible with other key players in the system, especially the reporter and children's panel members. The use of diversion and the application of the principle of 'minimum necessary intervention' within a welfare-based system is both complex and controversial. There is a 'conceptual ambiguity' about diverting young people from welfare that is less of an issue in a natural justice context. For this reason, it is even more essential that key players within the local system have a shared understanding of the ethos of 'minimum necessary intervention' and adopt agreed strategies for its practical implementation at a local level. The aim would be to ensure that diverting children and young people from compulsory supervision does not mean failing to meet their needs.

The great advantage in a locally focused multi-agency approach to juvenile justice is described and illustrated by Rutherford (1988) and the very great danger of practising systems intervention without engaging effectively with other parts of the system is illustrated throughout 'The Report of the Inquiry into Child Care Policies in Fife' (Kearney, 1992).

This latter report contains the following quote by Lockyer (1988), commenting on the divergence between SBR recommendations and hearing outcomes in the Region of Fife:

> The question which the entire analysis raises and begs is what degree of agreement or divergence is acceptable or 'healthy'? Clearly there must be a level of unacceptable disagreement. In Fife, where recommendations and decisions 'to discharge' are at such variance that the advice to discharge is as likely to be rejected as accepted, there seems to be a fundamental disagreement between the parties about the value of compulsory care in general. It cannot be desirable for such opposing views to exist – irrespective of whose view prevails.

Conclusion

A study which focuses on outcomes cannot give a satisfactory explanation as to why differential outcomes occur – this requires a more qualitative approach, focused on the processes involved in decision-making, the values, attitudes and beliefs of the key actors, and the nature and influence of 'team culture' or 'ethos'. Differences in outcome may be, to some extent, inevitable in a system of juvenile justice which is based on welfare, discretion and individualized decision-making. However, we must surely ask whether the wide discrepancies in outcome suggested by this study do not indicate the potential for injustice, or, excessive intervention, into the lives of young people and their families.

The use of ARGs may help to ensure a more consistent and 'minimum necessary' approach, and does seem to lead to greater use of IT as a resource. However, it may be equally valuable to harness the informal processes of a team by influencing the values of the 'team culture'. These two approaches are not, of course, mutually exclusive. In addition, diversionary outcomes may be more effectively promoted by engaging other key players in the local system, for example: the use of local multi-agency forums to negotiate issues such as the use of the police warning system; the appropriate content of SBR reports; criteria for the application of 'minimum necessary intervention' at different stages in a child care career; and establishing shared systems for the monitoring and review of decision-making in the local system. A negotiated understanding of what is meant by 'minimum necessary intervention' may help all parties to agree on the value of compulsory measures of care, as well as establishing a shared understanding of when diversion is the most appropriate outcome.

Paradoxically, although diversion and systems management are often promoted as ways of ensuring greater equity of outcome between different geographical areas, strategies to implement diversion are probably most effective when negotiated between key actors in the system at a local level (Rutherford, 1988).

References

Bottoms, A. and Stelman, A. (1988) *Social Enquiry Reports: A Framework for Practice Development*. Community Care Practice Handbooks. Wildwood House.

Burns, T. and Stalker, G.M. (1966) *The Management of Innovation*. London: Tavistock.

DHSS (1985) *Social Work Decisions in Child Care: Recent Research Findings and their Implications*. London: HMSO.

Fuller, R. and Petch, A. (1991) Does area team organisation make a difference?, *British Journal of Social Work*, 21: 471–89.

Intermediate Treatment Resource Centre (1986) *Review of IT in Scotland: Part 1 – National Report*. Glasgow: ITRC.

Kearney, B. (1992) *The Report of the Inquiry into Child Care Policies in Fife*. Edinburgh: HMSO.

Lockyer, A. (1988) *Study of Children's Hearings' Disposals in Relation to Resources*. Children's Panel Chairman's Group.

Martin, F.M., Fox, S.J. and Murray, K. (1981) *Children Out of Court*. Edinburgh: Scottish Academic Press.

Morris, A. and McIsaac, M. (1978) *Juvenile Justice*. London: Heinemann.

Morris, A., Giller, H., Szwed, E. and Geach, H. (1980) *Justice for Children*. London: Macmillan.

Peters, T.J. and Waterman, R.H. (1982) *In Search of Excellence: Lessons from America's Best Run Companies*. New York: Harper and Row.

Raynor, P. (1993) Systems purists, client refusal and gatekeeping: is help necessarily harmful?, *Social Action*, 1: 4–8.

Rutherford, A. (1988) The next step, in Doyle, S. *Towards a Custody Free Community*. Association for Juvenile Justice.

Scottish Office (1993) Referrals of children to Reporters and children's hearings 1991. *Statistical Bulletin: Social Work Series*. Edinburgh: Government Statistical Service.

Social Services Inspectorate (1988) *Decentralisation of Social Services Departments: Project Report No. 2*. DHSS.

Social Work Services Group (1987) *Compulsory Measures of Care for Children: Home Supervision*. Edinburgh: SWSG.

Strathclyde Regional Council (1985) *The Care Strategy for Young People in Trouble*. Strathclyde Regional Council.

Thorpe, D.H., Smith, D., Green, C.J. and Paley, J.H. (1980) *Out of Care: The Community Support of Juvenile Offenders*. London: Allen and Unwin.

Tutt, N. and Giller, H. (1984a) *Diversion*. Lancaster: Social Information Systems. [Audio-tape]

Tutt, N. and Giller, H. (1984b) *Social Inquiry Reports*. Lancaster: Social Information Systems. [Audio-tape]

Vernon, J. and Fruin, D. (1986) *In Care: a Study of Social Work Decision Making*. London: National Children's Bureau.

Chapter 7

The social work role with personality-disordered clients

Anne Irvine
Grampian Social Work Department

Introduction

Interest in this topic arose as a result of the increasing referrals to the Community Mental Heath Team of clients who had a diagnosis of 'personality disorder'. This team was created from a departmental reorganization and constituted a recognition of the fact that adults with mental health problems were not receiving an adequate service from the social work department. It was hoped that this client group's needs could be more adequately met by the provision of a team where workers could prioritize clients in the community suffering from mental health problems. Whilst we work with individuals who have a psychiatric history, we also see individuals who are not receiving help from the psychiatric services, but who experience the range of mental health problems.

The team held a workshop in 1989 where the alarming increase in referrals of clients with the diagnosis 'personality disorder' was noted over the past three years. The team concluded that this client group experienced a wide range of social and emotional problems and were not in receipt of help from other agencies. They appeared to take up a lot of social work time with apparently little improvement in their circumstances and a tendency to demand ongoing long-term involvement. Many clients were known to have a history of institutional care and had been discharged into the community with few obvious support networks from either services or professionals.

The overall aim was to examine the social work role in relation to people with personality disorders, and to find out what kinds of work were being undertaken with clients. Implicit in this was the hope that the research would enable the team to formulate a clearer policy for working with this client group.

There were four main research questions in my examination of the social work role with this client group.

1 How do these clients arrive at the social work department?
2 What problems do these clients experience?
3 What kinds of work are social workers doing with these clients?
4 How are they doing it?

I shall begin with a brief description of the diagnosis 'personality disorder' in order to further set the scene for my study. The main part of the report describes the sample and findings, and works through the four research questions. This is followed by a discussion of findings and concluding remarks.

What exactly is a personality disorder?

The British Classification of Psychiatric Illnesses (CD-10) and the American one (DSM-IIIR) provide detailed categorizations of personality disorders and their traits. The label itself is loaded with negative implications and is both unpleasant and stigmatizing for clients. Articles in the *British Medical Journal* in recent years discuss the problems in making this diagnosis and stress the fact that it is a socially undesirable diagnosis. Sims (1990) states that most personality disorders are disorders of behaviour and are largely caused by psychosocial factors. Tyrer (1990) highlights the links between stressful life events and a diagnosis of personality disorder. He is of the opinion that therapeutic interventions can be effective but that new approaches to its treatment are required.

Characteristically, clients with this diagnosis are noted for their 'difficult behaviour'. Often there is evidence of a disadvantaged childhood including significant losses and institutional care. Lack of ability to form lasting emotional attachments and an inability to empathize with others and view the world outside themselves are common. Unpredictable, destructive, manipulative and addictive behaviours are often present along with lack of insight and an inability to learn from past experiences.

I do not wish to debate the advantages, or lack of them, of making this diagnosis which is so highly emotive. What I wish to concentrate on are the particular difficulties this client group experience with a view to facilitating better service planning for the group. In recent years, psychiatric hospitals have tended not to class this diagnosis as a clinical mental illness, and hence not treatable in the established sense. This has implications for those clients who have often previously been dependent on in-patient psychiatric services when they are in crisis.

The 1986 Mental Welfare Commission Report highlighted 'difficult' cases, and their lack of suitable supports. Following this, Lothian Region researched a sample of cases which were perceived as 'difficult' and again, most of these involved clients with a 'personality disorder' diagnosis (Buglass, 1988). Both these sources noted the gaps in services for this client group and highlighted the particular problems they experience.

I could only find one piece of social work literature which focused on this client group (Burton, 1990). This possibly reflects a reluctance to accept the personality disorder label and to stigmatize by creating another 'client group'. However, I believe that this group do have particular problems which need to be examined in the context of their 'diagnosis' in order that services can be developed to meet their particular needs.

Methodology

The sample group consisted of 30 cases where clients had a diagnosis of personality disorder. All but three were held by workers in the Community Mental Health Team. Those three were held by a hospital-based social worker. The sample comprised cases which were currently open, and those which were closed within the past year (as at May 1991). My initial intention had been to obtain half of the sample cases from social workers based in the local psychiatric hospital. However, after preliminary examination it transpired that very few cases were held by hospital workers and that the Community Mental Health Team was working with the bulk of these clients who presented for help. Three cases were included from a hospital worker to increase the sample to 30.

The research focused on social workers' views of their work with clients. I had hoped to incorporate an element of client opinion, but was unable to include this for reasons of time.

There were two data sources for the project. A lengthy questionnaire was completed for each client, and an interview with social workers in the Community Mental Health Team was completed. Both were piloted, albeit on a limited basis.

The questionnaire collated mainly quantitative data on the sample cases (age, housing, history of institutional care, reason for referral, other agencies involved) but also focused on more qualitative information concerned with degree of social isolation, methods of work used, and effectiveness of intervention indicators. The questionnaire was based on the much utilized Goldberg case review form and was extended and adapted (Goldberg and Warburton, 1979). Most of the questions have been used in other areas of social work research and have been tested for reliability. Much of the data here was gained from case files.

The interview schedule asked a series of open and closed questions and aimed to collate qualitative data on the methods of work used by social workers, problems experienced in working with these clients and positive suggestions for the 'way forward' with the client group. I interviewed all the workers and completed the schedules during the interviews which lasted between 30 minutes and $1\frac{1}{4}$ hours.

Both the questionnaires and interview schedules were completed over July and August 1991.

Main findings

Description of sample

The sample totalled 30 clients. Twenty of these were women and ten were men. There was a noticeable age cluster for females with 60 per cent being in their thirties. Male ages ranged evenly from their twenties to their fifties. Almost 50 per cent of female clients lived with their partner or family, contrasting with less than 25 per cent of the men. Conversely, 50 per cent of male clients lived alone, while only 20 per cent of female clients did so. The remainder of the sample either lived with friends, fellow boarders, hostel residents or patients. Only 10 per cent of the sample were resident in hostel accommodation of a supported nature. Eighty-two per cent of clients were dependent on state benefits for their income and two clients were in current employment at the time the study was conducted. Two-thirds of the sample were from the Aberdeenshire area.

Only 3 per cent of clients did not have a history of institutional care. Fifty-five per cent had experience of living in children's homes/foster care and 85 per cent of in-patient treatment in psychiatric hospitals. Nearly 50 per cent of the sample had spent more than ten years in institutional care, with only 15 per cent having spent less than one year in institutional care. Forty-eight per cent had been in contact with the social work department most of their lives and had been allocated to a number of social workers in various departments throughout the country.

How did these clients arrive at the social work department?

Thirty per cent of clients were referred by other social work departments to the team, and another 25 per cent by hospital-based social workers. Twenty per cent referred themselves. Almost 25 per cent were referred by hospital doctors and community-based nursing staff, although none was referred by their GP. The remainder came via the police, court or relatives. Fifty per cent had had more than three previous social work allocations which were known about; in reality there had probably been many more given that almost half of the sample had been known to social work departments most of their lives. Only one client was a completely new referral to social work, although four clients were new referrals to Aberdeen social work services.

Reason for referral

These were divided into primary and secondary reasons for referral. Workers were asked to tick two primary reasons but could identify any number of secondary reasons for referral.

Primary reasons

In 50 per cent of cases, mental health problems was one of the two primary reasons for referral. Behavioural difficulties and relationship/emotional difficulties constituted another 40 per cent of primary reasons.

Secondary reasons

Concern over welfare, housing, financial and relationship/emotional difficulties were all ranked equally and constituted over 80 per cent of secondary reasons for referral. General support/advice and social work assessment were also significantly common reasons.

What problems were this group experiencing?

Social workers were asked to identify the problems they had tackled with their clients. The three most common problems which social workers tackled were:

1 Emotional distress.
2 Relationship/family problems.
3 Housing.

However, loneliness or social isolation, financial or material problems, home-care issues and vulnerability to exploitation followed closely as other problems which were being addressed.

In almost two-thirds of cases, social isolation was identified as a problem worthy of attention. Interestingly, in almost 50 per cent of cases where clients lived with their partner/family, social isolation was still identified as a problem, and it appeared that this group had almost no social contacts outwith their immediate family. Ten per cent of clients had no social contacts at all and 45 per cent of those who did not live with their family saw their extended family less than fortnightly. One-third of clients had contact with friends/neighbours on a weekly basis. However, it was noticeable that family and friends constituted the main regular social contacts for clients. Only three clients regularly attended a day centre or drop-in facility and only one client made use of a community centre. Whilst the data illustrated that two-thirds of clients made use of day centres, church or community resources on an occasional basis, it was not possible to determine if this was once a month or once a year. Suffice to say that community resources were not utilized on any regular basis by the vast majority of this client group at this point in time.

Housing

'Housing' in its broadest sense was identified as a problem for two-thirds of the sample. A common view held within the team was that this client group experienced tremendous housing problems. The interview schedule highlighted the point that many clients viewed attaining a council tenancy as the solution to all their problems; unfortunately, they tended to have very unrealistic ideas about what managing a tenancy involved.

Neighbour problems were commonly named as creating great difficulties for clients in sustaining a tenancy. Social isolation, practicalities such as budgeting for bills, and furnishing a tenancy, along with their tendency to make unreasonable demands on others, were also highlighted as areas of difficulty. Despite this, 40 per cent of the sample had their own council tenancy and length of stay ranged from six months to over two years. However, those who were able to maintain tenancies often did so by the 'skin of their teeth'; social isolation and being placed in hard to let areas were cited as the two main reasons for the almost inevitable problems with neighbours which these clients encountered.

Another main point to emerge from the interview schedules was that social workers felt there was a great gap in suitable accommodation for clients with severe behavioural difficulties. It was this group which appeared to have most problems with securing and maintaining suitable accommodation and for whom it was felt there were no resources at the moment. Only 10 per cent of the sample were resident in supported accommodation (i.e. hostels), none was resident in group homes, private rented properties or housing association tenancies. Forty per cent of clients lived variously in bed and breakfast accommodation, with friends or extended family (effectively no fixed abode for many) and a further 10 per cent were resident in the state hospital, Carstairs.

All the social workers interviewed stated that there were neither sufficient nor suitable housing resources for this client group, particularly for those with severe behavioural problems. Hostels were seen as useful for client assessment, and reducing social isolation, but because of the particular difficulties which these clients pose in terms of their demanding behaviour and chaotic lifestyle, it was felt that a special hostel could benefit this group of clients. A common problem for those who had been in hostels on a short-term basis was that placements failed, often through clients being unable to adhere to hostel rules. On a few occasions, clients had been denied access to some supported accommodation options because 'personality disorder' was not seen as a mental illness. Thirty per cent of the sample lived completely alone, another one-third lived with family/friends and the remainder lived with fellow boarders, residents or patients. Housing was the primary reason for a referral in 15 per cent of cases, and rose to 20 per cent as a secondary reason. Whilst two-thirds of clients were viewed by their social workers as being suitably housed, part of this response was due to the lack of suitable types of supported accommodation. The two main reasons cited for unsuitability of existing accommodation were the range of problems these clients have in managing a tenancy, and the general lack of resources for those with severe behavioural problems.

Did this client group have particular housing needs?

In general, it was felt that those clients who need a more supported living environment were not being catered for. Whilst it is difficult for clients to be allocated a tenancy and they encounter a range of problems in holding onto this tenancy, it was felt that their needs were not vastly different to other client groups who are trying to live independently for the first time. That is, similar supports are needed. What is different is that their behaviour often precludes them from being able to sustain an independent tenancy, yet they may be forced into the position of accepting one as no other suitable forms of accommodation are on offer – the alternative to this often being bed and breakfast accommodation which tends to be very insecure and temporary.

Social workers stated that for some clients who had their own tenancy, this created an additional source of stress and anxiety for them. Some were placed in hard-to-let areas where there was evidence of ex-psychiatric patient 'ghettos' and where the more vulnerable clients were often exploited. This tended to increase their level of emotional distress and consequently made it harder for the workers to enable them to manage independently. I have already quoted figures stating the high degree of institutional care which this sample has experienced and this, plus their interpersonal and behavioural difficulties, ensure that the odds are not in their favour when they do try to manage a tenancy. A tremendous amount of social work and home-care support is needed to facilitate success in this form of accommodation. It was felt that a more flexible approach and greater understanding of their difficulties was needed by the housing department. The questionnaire showed that the housing department was involved with two-thirds of cases in the sample. However, there was regular contact between the social worker and this department in only 25 per cent of this number. It may be that improved communication in this area could facilitate earlier warning of housing problems and earlier intervention may prevent problems becoming intractable.

I have concentrated on housing as a major problem for this client group as it appears to be crucial in determining whether workers feel they can be effective in their interventions. Workers commonly stated that they were more able to help clients with relationship problems and their emotional difficulties if their living circumstances were stable, housing constituting a major contributory factor in whether their circumstances were stable. This is no surprise, and it has long been a view in social work practice that it is not possible to help clients with emotional difficulties until their basic needs for shelter and food have been met.

Just as lack of appropriate supported housing was viewed as a major problem for this client group, lack of suitable day-care options was similarly highlighted. This is borne out by the negligible use of existing facilities by this client group.

How were social workers working with this client group?

The three most commonly used methods of work were: general support/advice/advocacy; client-centred counselling; and task-centred work with use of contracts. Crisis intervention and behavioural approaches were also used to a significant degree. In almost 40 per cent of cases it was recorded that no task-centred work was used. This can be linked to the 70 per cent of cases where social workers found it difficult or extremely difficult to use the CASER (Client Access and Ethical Recording System) system of contract-based work. The CASER system of initial and review contracts was only viewed as easy to use in one of the 30 cases. The main difficulties in using the CASER system were the difficulty in getting the client to understand it – many clients were suspicious of written documents and others simply could not grasp the intention behind it. Furthermore, the fact that clients' presenting problems were constantly fluctuating meant that contracts were often invalid soon after they had been completed. The third main difficulty with CASER was the client's lack of commitment to overcoming their problems.

The interview schedules highlighted the point that client motivation to work on their problems tended to be, at best, temporary. This client group are not 'long-term thinkers', and often do not see themselves and their behaviour as problematic, but instead believe that others are the source of their problems. Whilst most clients recognized that they had difficulties, it was their disagreement on the nature of these which made CASER so difficult to operate.

The one positive aspect of CASER was that it could be useful in defining realistic expectations of social work intervention for the client. However, the system does not enable much of the counselling work and often daily 'maintenance' intervention which goes on to be noted. As most clients have been through the range of state welfare systems they often experienced CASER as threatening, bureaucratic and impersonal. Other client groups may find CASER a useful way of facilitating joint planning between worker and client. This client group seem unable to commit themselves to the idea of a contract; they often agree to it at the time then forget about it, and do not understand its relevance.

Workers felt that they could formulate clear objectives in their work but stated that it was very easy to lose sight of these objectives, as clients found it almost impossible to formulate aims along with them. Getting the clients' attention for long enough to look at objectives was a major problem because of their inability to think beyond the immediacy of their situation. This difficulty was compounded by their day-to-day problems constantly changing in terms of what they viewed as 'problematic'.

The social worker/client relationship was viewed as important in almost all cases. Workers acknowledged that clients tended to use social work support on their terms, but it was felt that some were able to use the relationship to learn and to trust, and very much valued someone taking a genuine interest in them – even if there was nothing that could be done to improve their situation. In many cases, the social worker was the only professional willing to spend time listening to them and trying to help, and this was viewed as very useful in enabling them to continue functioning in the community.

A major use of the relationship as a therapeutic tool was as a role model of consistency. The need for total consistency when working with this client group is widely acknowledged.

Significantly, day centres and daytime activities were areas where workers felt they could do little to help. Often clients had tried to use the range of services on offer but their involvement was rarely tolerated on an ongoing basis. Given their high level of social isolation, this raises the other question of what should be provided for this group. It emerged that the social worker constitutes an important social contact for many clients. Lamentable as this is, it has to be looked at in considering long-term work with this client group. Most workers felt that the client group needed long-term social work input. Ongoing work may be done on a crisis or short-term basis but consistent long-term involvement was an important factor in enabling them to function in the community, and care management was facilitated by the same worker remaining involved to avoid manipulation of new workers.

Two-thirds of the sample displayed aggressiveness, or verbal abuse, and almost 80 per cent were known for their unpredictable behaviour. Despite this, social workers felt that a good relationship with the client enabled these behaviours to be contained. At times this meant the worker coping with a lot of misdirected anger and aggression, and it is here that colleague support and supervision is vital in ensuring that the worker places appropriate limits on their relationship. This also raises the issue of when a worker should withdraw, the overall view being that when client anger and manipulation became excessive they must be given the clear message that their behaviour is unacceptable. This may pose a dilemma for workers who are aware of the client's own vulnerability and awareness to exploitation and makes it more difficult to close a case when there is no reasonable possibility of working being done. Despite this client group's history and need for help they do tend to be 'survivors' and workers should not overestimate the importance of their relationship with clients. Their coping mechanisms may be maladaptive, but do enable them to 'muddle through' when the occasion arises. The neediness of these clients should not cloud the workers' awareness of their unpredictability and potential risks to their own safety.

Views were mixed concerning whether these clients could be worked with on a short-term basis. In this sample, cases tended to be open for a short time only when there were difficulties with the client (e.g. totally uncooperative), or when the client moved away. Otherwise cases inevitably remained open in the longer term. Most workers felt that long-term involvement was necessary because of the nature of clients' difficulties. However, it was also felt that whilst long-term involvement was needed, work was more feasible on a short-term basis. Cases tended to remain open due to continuing crises rather than planned long-term treatment goals. Social work interventions were concentrated around these times of crisis and contact in between depended largely on the cooperativeness of clients.

The interview schedule asked workers to list problems they felt they could help clients with, and those they felt they could do little or nothing about. Most of the problems appeared in both lists, and a major factor in determining whether problems could be alleviated concerned the client's level of ability to work along with the social worker. Many clients were viewed as creating constant crises in their lives, and often had unrealistic expectations of what social work could do to help. Their individual level of impetuousness and tendency to sabotage work plans were other main factors in determining effectiveness of intervention.

Half of the sample was seen on a weekly basis and a quarter every two weeks. A small percentage were seen more than twice per week, and a similar number were seen less than fortnightly. In all but one of the cases, visits were planned, either in the office or at the client's house. However, in almost one-third of cases, the client often attended the office unannounced. Interviews tended to be the standard 50 minutes or else very short (when unplanned). It is these unplanned visits which give workers the impression that these clients take up 'too much' of their time. All the workers felt that regular, time-limited appointments were crucial with this group. Client non-attendance, followed by turning up unannounced, was a major frustration, but seen as important in helping them to learn about limits. Time was viewed as being ineffectively spent when the same tasks were repeatedly being performed, e.g. finding bed and breakfast accommodation. Many workers did feel that they wasted time pursuing strategies which they felt were doomed to failure. At times this was done to maximize chances of helping the client ('maybe it will work out this time') or at the request of other professionals. Experience with this client group was seen as important in determining whether strategies were tried. Workers felt more confident in saying 'no' and setting limits as they gained experience with individual clients and this client group.

Workers were asked about cases where they felt there had been a positive outcome. Examples included: keeping client out of prison; some change in antisocial behaviour; non-professional support gained; material improvement. There were mixed views regarding whether more 'successful' cases were functioning at a higher level to begin with. Others felt that client willingness to work with them was more important in being effective than their level of functioning. Cases where workers felt they were less effective included instances of the following: clients with too many dependencies (e.g. alcohol or drugs); client not motivated to change; lifestyle too chaotic to work with on any consistent basis.

Social work activities

Liaison, investigation or assessment, and information or advice giving were the most common social work activities. However, facilitating problem-solving, counselling, advisory and mobilizing resources were engaged in to much the same extent. Despite the fact that liaison with other agencies and professionals was cited amongst the top three social work activities, in almost one-third of cases there was no *regular* contact with others involved. GPs, housing department and out-patient psychiatric services were most commonly involved with clients, and also constituted those agencies who were liaised with on a regular basis. It should also be noted that there are particular problems relating to GPs as some clients were not registered with a GP, and others had been struck off numerous GP lists.

There were 13 voluntary agencies involved with the clients, along with other service providers such as DSS, and it would seem that it is with these agencies that there tends to be less liaison. Often social workers are not aware that their clients are involved and some clients have a tendency to try the range of voluntary sector agencies for support or material help. Social workers felt that clients were usually seen as a nuisance and a waste of time by other agencies. However, it was also commonly experienced that clients were initially seen as vulnerable by other agencies, and it was not until they had taken advantage of or abused these agencies that social workers became aware of clients' involvement with them. Other voluntary agencies tended to have unrealistic expectations of the social worker's role, especially where the client had been manipulative and/or was seen by them as vulnerable. This 'criticism' was seen as exacerbating the feelings of isolation which social workers often experience when working with this client group.

Social workers were the only professionals who had regular contact in 90 per cent of cases. Workers stated that there were both advantages and disadvantages of them being the main professional. The main advantage was that there were no other professionals who could be manipulated. However, this was outnumbered by the disadvantages. Some workers felt isolated and unsupported, especially if outside agencies were pressuring them. Others felt that it would be very useful if a GP were involved as great problems were created when a client was very distressed and it would have been useful if there was a named psychiatrist who knew the patient and who could give advice when needed. In the few cases where this was on offer, it was seen as beneficial.

Workers did not feel there were other professionals who were better placed to work with these clients but some would value the use of hospital for short-term admissions when their client became too distressed to function in the community. Given the institutional history of most of the sample, I wonder if it is entirely fair for psychiatric hospitals to refuse admissions due to clients' diagnoses, given their history of institutional care and psychiatric admissions.

Services provided

In only one case was it recorded that no services were provided to the client, and in this case, making initial contact proved so difficult that the case was closed. Financial help and assistance with form-filling were the services most commonly provided, with homemaker support, other material help and referral to other agencies for assessment being similarly common.

Of the range of psychological help given, those most commonly used were clarification of the real situation, ventilation of feelings and general emotional support. In 50 per cent of cases, social workers stated that they spent equal amounts of time doing counselling and practical work. In 45 per cent of cases, social workers felt that change had occurred on a temporary basis, although the client's situation remained largely the same, and in 42 per cent of cases social workers felt that some positive change had been achieved in some areas.

Discussion

The particular features of this sample confirmed ideas already held within the team about the background these clients have and the problems they encounter. The findings did highlight the long history of contact with the department which clients had, and for our department to deny a service to this client group seems harsh, given their previous involvement with us.

Social isolation and lack of suitable daytime activities posed a major problem for workers in trying to help these clients. They rarely use existing mental health day centres or local projects on any regular basis. However, they are known to a range of local agencies and some clients regularly used day-care resources for the homeless. A major difficulty with their current use of day-care services is that they tend to be banned because of behavioural difficulties. This could be a fruitful area for more formal liaison in order that their behaviour is contained wherever possible and use of the resource is maintained.

Much of the literature discussing this diagnosis emphasizes the importance of consistency in treatment. Burton (1990) stresses that a therapeutic relationship must be based on consistency and focus on the problem behaviours rather than the 'label' of personality disorder. It is vital that other agencies working with our clients, whenever possible (even on a sporadic basis) are liaised with in order that a consistent response to problem behaviours is maintained and the clients' potential for positive change facilitated.

The Scottish Association of Mental Health paper on community care policy of 1989 emphasized the need to take seriously the significant effect of homelessness on mental health. Housing was the third most common problem which clients in this sample experienced. Whilst an encouragingly high percentage did have council tenancies, there were often constant problems in helping them sustain the tenancy. Few of them lived in supported accommodation and on occasions had been denied access because of their diagnosis. Given their history of institutional care, they require a high level of support and advice in this area. Workers stated that their casework was much more effective when a client's housing situation was stable. Those with severe behavioural problems had greatest difficulty in sustaining any stable accommodation and it seems vital that their needs be examined in relation to developing housing initiatives in the community. If clients are 'failing' in existing forms of supported accommodation because of their inability to adhere to accepted rules, then serious consideration must be given to developing a resource which will meet their needs.

Despite workers' feelings that they were 'doing' little with these clients, the results highlighted the range of social work methods and services being used. Importance was placed on the social worker/client relationship as a therapeutic tool and the need for consistency of worker and of their methods emphasized. It is tempting to suggest that these clients cannot be worked with on a long-term basis because of their impetuosity and inability to commit themselves to working agreements. Results revealed the importance of one worker being available to clients in the long term in order that their tendency to manipulate is lessened. Burton (1990) believes that we do these clients a distinct disservice by seeing them on an intake basis. This lends weight to the finding that these clients require consistent long-term involvement. It is recognized that many of this group use social work only when they are in a crisis situation (as they define it) but it seems important that, wherever possible, they have access to a social worker who knows them when they do present.

The findings suggest that social workers *are* engaged in useful work with clients. They point out that both counselling and more practical forms of help are being provided in roughly equal amounts and that positive change is achieved with many clients. It is tempting to believe that there is no reason for continued social work involvement if the client is unable to follow through on work plans and there is little change in their circumstances. However, the long-term nature of their problems must be considered, and despite the frustrations in working with them, it appears that useful social work is being done. As ever, the notion of social work 'effectiveness', *per se*, is elusive. Perhaps if these same clients were researched in ten years time, further indicators of their 'progress' would be more obvious.

Prior to this research, a main concern of team members was the apparently high proportion of their time which was being spent with this client group. The results indicated that workers only felt this group took up too much of their time when they were in a crisis, and that non-crisis contacts were of a similar frequency to other clients. I do not wish to detract from the many frustrations of working with these clients, as they are very real and can undermine workers' confidence and enthusiasm. Despite rising referrals of personality-disorder clients, they are still small in number, and it is possible to ensure that workers only have a few on their caseload.

Conclusions

This study set out to examine the social work role in relation to clients referred to the Community Mental Health Team with a diagnosis of 'personality disorder'. Much of it is descriptive and offers evidence of the problems these clients present with and how social workers are dealing with them. The main purpose was to collate information which the team could use in planning work with this client group.

The data illustrate that these clients are being referred appropriately, and that they encounter the range of social, emotional and practical problems. It is their particular behavioural and interpersonal difficulties which determine the specific problems they have in relation to social isolation, housing and productive daytime activity which need to be addressed. Tyrer (1989) highlights the link between stressful life events and the personality disorder diagnosis and emphasizes the need for support.

It is difficult to say precisely how effective social workers have been with these clients. What I hope to have shown is that we do provide them with a service which tries to alleviate their presenting problems. The research does provide some evidence of positive outcomes in work with this group. The Mental Welfare Commission (1986) report details the plight of behaviourally disordered clients and the dilemmas they pose for system.

I wish to conclude by listing particular points and questions raised from the study which, if tackled, could improve problem reduction for personality-disordered clients.

- There is a specific lack of suitable accommodation for clients with severe behavioural problems. I hope that this study adds to the evidence that specialist housing provision is needed for this group.
- Improved liaison with the housing department, both at the time of initial allocation and when problems arise, is needed if we are to prevent these clients from 'failing' in the community.
- There is still a need for psychiatric hospital to offer short-term 'asylum' for clients who have a history of in-patient treatment. Is it fair to deny clients this option when many have been 'treated' by this method in the past?
- Social isolation is a major problem, and there is a need to develop day-care services which could alleviate this. This group tend not to use mental health resources. When can existing services try and meet their needs?
- Many clients in this sample did not have a GP. Liaison with GPs to accept these clients on their lists would be advantageous, as some clients are currently denied a service which is a basic right.
- Despite other services often labelling these clients as 'unworkable with',

social work intervention can be effective. The social work role is crucial if these clients are to be enabled to function in the community, outwith the institutional environments where many of them have spent a significant proportion of their lives.

References

Buglass, D. (1988) 'Difficult Cases – The Lothian Scene', unpublished research paper. Lothian Region Social Work Department.

Burton, A. (1990) Personality disorder – the limits to intervention, *Practice*, 4: 4.

Goldberg, E.M. and Warburton, W. (1979) *Ends and Means in Social Work*. London: Allen and Unwin.

Mental Welfare Commission (1986) *Annual Report*.

Scottish Association for Mental Health (1989) *Government Policy on Community Care for People with Mental Health Problems in Scotland*.

Sims, A. (1990) Neuroses and personality disorders, *Current Opinion in Psychiatry*, 3: 179–81.

Tyrer, P. (1989) Clinical importance of personality disorder, *Current Opinion in Psychiatry*, 2: 240–3.

Tyrer, P. (1990) Diagnosing personality disorders, *Current Opinion in Psychiatry*, 3: 182–7.

Chapter 8

Preparing or deterring? Consumer feedback on preparation groups for prospective adoptive parents in Barnardo's Family Placement Project, Edinburgh

Sue MacFadyen
Barnardo's Family Placement Services

Introduction: background to the study

The bounds of possibility in adoption are getting harder to define. It *is* possible for children with all sorts of extra special needs and complexities to join and grow up in all sorts of new permanent families, as the achievements of many adoption agencies, including Family Placement Services, Edinburgh, demonstrate. This positive expansion of the field of adoption is confirmed by a majority of studies (e.g. Macaskill, 1985; Nelson, 1985; Borland *et al.*, 1989; Thoburn and Rowe, 1988), which have, in addition, challenged child care and adoption practice through their identification of the risk factors pertaining to the child at placement, such as age, number of previous moves or disruptions, loss of contact with the past and separation from siblings.

Interestingly, as Thoburn (1990) points out, equivalent risk factors in adopters or permanent carers have been harder to define from research, with only the common-sense issue of the degree of realism and acceptance within adoptive parents' expectations of the placement commanding any certainty. While the provision of group preparation for prospective adopters is an acknowledgement of the latter point, the continued traditional assessment process, with its assumption of an 'objective reality' definable by social workers (Ryburn, 1991), seems at variance with the former. Both preparation and assessment further refine the recruitment process, with assessment still carrying the greater influence. Yet, while the expanding art of the possible in adoption has opened up not just 'who can be adopted' but also 'who can adopt', the limits to recruitment nevertheless pose a major constraint on adoption. The fact of limitation is, of course, inevitable. Its degree may be less so: that is, not all current limitations imposed on the complete recruitment process may be necessary or relevant to 'good enough' adoption.

It was with these concerns as a backdrop that I wanted to look more closely at the preparation groups, run by Family Placement Services, for prospective adoptive and permanent carers. The provision of such group meetings, in which the process, demands and experience of special needs adoption are shared with applicants, is a well-established part of adoption practice (Horne, 1983; Smith, 1988). However, as Triseliotis (1988) points out, an original impetus behind this development – that of promoting self-selection by would-be adopters (Kirk, 1964) – has been muddied and diffused somewhat in practice. Triseliotis (1988: 22) notes the lack of evidence that 'any agency has put all its reliance on groups, abandoning the individual home study. Agencies seem to combine the two approaches.' This is certainly the position of Family Placement Services, where attendance at the groups is a first step in the continuing assessment process. As a starting point to reviewing the project's practice in this area, and in an attempt to bring some clarity to our thinking on the overlap or relationship between recruitment, preparation and assessment, I wanted to find out the degree to which, and ways in which, the groups contributed to the process of self-selection by participants.

In addition to evaluating the groups as 'recruitment filters', I also wanted to obtain feedback on the usefulness of groups as 'information providers' – on the structure and content of the group meetings, and their perceived relevance, both at the time and subsequently. Thus, I proposed to obtain feedback from users on two main questions:

1 How helpful and relevant is the content of the group meetings, and how well do the format and structure meet the needs of participants?
2 How much, and in what ways, do the groups help participants decide whether or not to continue with their application to adopt?

Planning the study: constraints and methodology

In preparing to undertake this evaluative research, several difficulties and limitations quickly became apparent.

- Family Placement Services is a small project, with four full-time adoption workers plus a Project Leader. The number of children placed each year (and therefore the number of families prepared and assessed) is small and variable (8–12 on average). The small scale of the project is compounded by the very long timescale in adoption work (from recruitment to placement takes 6–12 months on average and sometimes much longer) and by the fact that support to placements made previously constitutes 50 per cent of project work. Thus, the number of group participants who could be included in the study was very limited.

- The study proposed is retrospective in nature, and therefore relied on respondents' memory of the groups they had attended. Because of this, it was decided to exclude all those who had attended groups more than three years previously. This limitation, combined with those above, meant that the research population of those participants who progressed to placement numbered 13 in total, exactly half of the total number of families, post-placement (26), to whom the project provides active contact or support.

- The project holds preparation groups two or three times a year, according to need. Although the overall framework and aim remain constant, each series of groups is inevitably unique. Variables contributing to this include the number and composition of participants, the number of meetings per series and different group leaders per series. Thus, responses to the survey would be based on varying experiences of the preparation groups, with only few, and general, constants.

In view of these constraints, and in consideration of the type of information being sought, a qualitative approach to data collection seemed most appropriate. Within the small scale of the study, it was hoped that this method would permit a depth and range of exploration of the subject. Incorporating and responding to consumer feedback is essential to adoption practice in general, and has played a crucial part in the development of project work in particular.

Achieving the study: fieldwork

Access to the 13 families who had attended groups within the last three years, and who had a child (or children) placed with them, was relatively straightforward, since all were in regular contact with the project.

A semistructured interview schedule was drawn up covering the main areas to be evaluated but leaving opportunity for more specific or detailed responses. An explanatory letter was sent out first with interviews arranged subsequently by telephone. Interviews lasting $1-1\frac{1}{2}$ hours were conducted over a two-month period, by the writer, in respondents' homes. Eleven such interviews were carried out as two couples were unavailable over the period allocated. All 11 respondents were married couples (see summary below), and in each case both partners were present at the interview.

In order to gain as full an understanding as possible of the impact of the groups, particularly in terms of how they contributed to the decision-making and self-selection of participants (Question 2, above), I wanted to contact a comparative sample of those who had attended the groups over the same period, and who had then withdrawn. Access to this population, however, was fraught with difficulties. People approach the possibility of adopting a child with special needs for all kinds of reasons. For many people, these reasons are underpinned to a greater or lesser extent by personal and painful loss: loss of a child; childlessness, whether in a first or subsequent marriage or partnership; loss of a relationship; loss of natural children to adulthood; loss by being turned down by other adoption agencies. This is not to imply that adoption is merely a second best, as for many 'new families' it is very much a positive choice. Nevertheless, particularly at the outset, issues of loss are part of the reality of adoption.

Thus, in attempting to contact people who had withdrawn, I was aware of the potential for re-awakening painful feelings in the individual or couple, while being unable to provide them with a service in return. In view of this, I decided that an explanatory letter, acknowledging some of the above accompanying a carefully worded questionnaire was most appropriate. The confidentiality of responses was stressed in both, and the questionnaire, echoing the semistructured interview schedule, focused on the process and content of the groups, leaving respondents free to include as much or as little personal information as they wished, or with the option of an interview. The total population who fulfilled the criteria was 19, comprising three single people and 16 couples.

A reminder letter and another copy of the questionnaire plus a stamped addressed envelope were sent out after a month. Of the 19, four letters and questionnaires were returned by the Post Office from the first mailing, and one from the second. Seven questionnaires were eventually completed, two by interview. All the returns were from couples. Thus single applicants are not represented in the study.

Analysis of main findings

For ease of organization and clarity, the information obtained has been collated and arranged under two categories, A and B.

Category	A Group participants post-placement	B Group participants who withdrew
Method	Semistructured interview, May/June	Postal questionnaire or interview, April/July
Possible	13	19
Actual	11	7 (2 interviewed)
Type	11 couples	7 couples

The structure, format and content of the groups

Overwhelmingly, the input to the groups by experienced adoptive parents was valued most highly by both categories (nine in category A; four in category B). This suggests that the project should consider making fuller use of adoptive parents' contribution, and involve them in the planning and co-leading of the groups. Hearing directly about what is involved in adoption from those who have achieved it enabled some respondents to put the rather daunting information provided into a more positive 'real-life' content:

A: 'The groups seem made to kind of put you off.'

B: 'People need reassurance at the beginning about who can adopt.'

Of the other methods of presenting information, only the small group experiential exercises produced a strong reaction, for or against, but with the majority very much in favour:

A: 'The exercise and issue about a child's past really struck home.'

Another main point around the organization of the meetings concerned the issue of time. While only three out of the total of 18 thought meeting others in a similar position was not helpful, ten of the remainder felt more time was needed to help group members relax, make acquaintance, and thus participate more in the discussion.

A: 'We would like more time to chat with others and learn from each other.'

A: 'We actually felt quite isolated and embarrassed because of the lack of opportunity to chat informally.'

B: 'We would have preferred more informal time to exchange views, fears, etc.'

In terms of the purpose of the groups, all respondents understood the importance of being given information about the demands and realities of adoption. However, in addition two couples in category A thought the groups were run primarily to allow the project to assess participants and 'eliminate' the unsuitable. As comments revealed, despite assurances to the contrary by project staff, several participants felt they were being tested or 'sized up':

A: 'If you can't cope with the groups, you certainly can't cope with the children.'

A: 'You feel you have to restrain yourself in case you say the wrong thing.'

In this, as in most other responses, category A couples were more outspoken and critical than category B couples, suggesting that, having achieved the goal of a child in placement, category A respondents could risk more candid feedback! This issue will be raised again when discussing the question of decision-making below, but the responses given hint at how undermining the experience of the groups may be, if even the 'successful' participants found them so testing. Further reinforcement of this comes from the three respondents – two from category B – who did not enjoy being in a group, and who indicated how undermined they felt by the experience.

B: 'The other people seemed to have children of their own, we were the only childless couple there, it wasn't helpful to us.'

Responses to questions about the usefulness of the content of the groups were almost as varied and numerous as the participants themselves (12 different answers from 18 respondents). This suggests that a broad range of issues should be covered to meet the variety of needs and experience represented. Given the mix of participants, this is a difficult task, since what was 'rather basic' to one couple was 'too intense and too much' for others.

The other main point in this area reveals the shortcomings of the questions asked. That ten couples, across both categories could cite 'nothing in particular' for what had been least helpful, is perhaps not surprising, given that they were being asked to remember the unmemorable! A more worthwhile question, hinted at by some general comments such as

A: 'There was too much emphasis on the difficulties.'

would have sought explicit feedback on the balance between encouragement and explanations of the problems inherent in adoption.

Similarly, the rationale for selecting category A respondents was that, in having a child placed with them (as opposed to those who had progressed only to assessment or who were approved and waiting for a child), they could provide some indication as to which information from the groups most resonated with the reality of caring for children with special needs. In practice, little information was gained from this question, and several couples commented on how hard it was to answer.

'In hindsight, yes, I suppose the groups have been helpful, but at the time we weren't really listening.'

This point will be further elaborated in the discussion below.

The role of the groups in the decision-making and self-selection of the participants

As stated above, one of the main reasons for holding groups at the beginning stages is to enable people to make an informed decision as to whether to proceed or not. This rather neat assumption by professionals is challenged by the results of this survey. All but one of the category A couples stated emphatically that they had already decided they wanted to adopt before attending the groups:

'We could have been put off by the groups but were determined to go ahead.'

'We had already made up our minds and went to the groups because it was part of what we had to do.'

'The meetings gave us more understanding of what's involved, but we had already decided and wouldn't be put off unless people said "no".'

In making sense of this finding, account must be taken of the possible distortion inherent in the long-term retrospective nature of the study. Nevertheless, the near unanimity of the responses – and in the remaining couple, one partner was fully decided on adoption prior to attending – demands that this finding should not easily be overlooked. Certainly, on the basis of these responses, it would seem that the preparation groups play no positive part in the decision-making and self-selection of the great majority of participants who do proceed to adoption. Indeed, most responded in terms of holding to their decision despite their experience of the groups.

Without doubt, to achieve their goal, adoptive parents must jump through many hoops while demonstrating much determination and perseverance. It would seem that, rather than serving to facilitate decision-making, preparation groups, as currently experienced, may do little more than set a first obstacle or test to participants (as their earlier responses indicated!). At the very least, this finding does not confirm a positive role for the groups in the process of applicant self-selection.

That the groups may help people to decide *not* to proceed, however, is partially confirmed by the mixed responses from category B. Four felt the groups had helped them a lot in their decision; one couple thought they had already decided to continue infertility treatment before attending; one couple felt the groups had only contributed a little to their decision; and the final couple were undecided. So to state it another way, while the groups did not deter the determined, neither did they encourage the uncertain.

A further factor relating to the composition of the two categories may be pertinent here. In category A – couples who progressed to placement – six of the 11 had children of their own. In a further two cases, one or both partners had children by a previous marriage. Only three couples were childless. Although the numbers involved are too tiny to act as indicators, nevertheless the majority of couples proceeding beyond the preparation groups were those who already had experience of, and were confident in, themselves as parents.

By contrast, only two of category B respondents – those couples who withdrew after the groups – had children. The remaining five couples were childless – one couple voluntarily so. Of those five couples, one had conceived since attending the groups, and a further two, including the voluntarily childless couple, after completing and returning the questionnaire, contacted the project and indicated their wish to continue with their application to adopt. Thus, although the seven respondents in category B may not be at all representative of the total possible population of 19, it is of note that the further contact initiated by the project and necessitated only by this survey was all the encouragement two couples required to renew their application!

This point relates to another area of the findings which links the format and structure of the groups to their assumed decision-making function. This concerns the opportunity (or lack of it) to meet privately with a project worker during the period the groups are running. For logistical and resource reasons, the project does not presently offer this, although participants are informed that a meeting can be set up if they so desire. This arrangement was seen as less than satisfactory by most respondents – seven category A, five category B:

A: 'We found ourselves trying to squeeze a moment privately with the social worker. Also having a meeting would let families know that support by the project is freely available.'

A: 'We wanted a separate meeting as we were afraid to ask in the group in case we looked silly.'

B: 'We would have liked to discuss our situation privately after the last meeting.'

The fact that the further contact from the project to group members who did not proceed resulted in two couples renewing their application, suggests it may be in the project's as well as the participants' interests to make such meetings more readily available.

What does it mean? Implications and recommendations

At its inception, an aim of this study had been to bring clarity to the idea of self-selection and to the links between preparation and assessment. At first glance, it might seem that only further confusion and complication have been achieved. Of the two main purposes of the groups – to provide applicants with information and to help them decide – the findings allow a rather insipid acknowledgement of the former, and a distinctly negative interpretation of the latter. However, the implications of the study can be very lively, but only if the present ambivalent or half-way house approach to the relationship between preparation and assessment is jettisoned in favour of a more radical embrace of applicant empowerment. If it can be, then the purposes of the groups can be rewritten along the lines suggested by users' responses: to facilitate the learning and development of prospective adopters and to support and share in their processes of self-assessment.

Parenting another's child is a complex task, different in many obvious and subtle ways from parenting a birth child. Special needs adoption brings many challenges and demands in its wake. It is, therefore, important that prospective adopters enter the process with as much understanding and awareness as possible. However, apart from those people – and there are many – who approach adoption with excess amounts of the necessary fortitude and flair, most others will require their portion to be nurtured and supported, and not snuffed out prematurely. This is most likely to be achieved if the educative and preparatory process is arranged as a partnership and if prospective adoptive parents are encouraged and permitted – with the lessening of the monopoly of 'professional' assessment – to assume as much control as possible over their learning process. That this can be achieved, with an accompanying increase in the quality of experience and preparation for all concerned, is evidenced by Stevenson (1991) and Ryburn (1991). Ryburn (1991: 25) writes:

> We acted in the belief that adoptive parenting is parenting plus and that what prospective adopters therefore needed was a programme which allowed them to test out and to learn, in order to come to their own conclusions. We were committed to the idea that today's 'not-good-enough adopters' by some formal assessment process, could become so with the right help and support.

From this philosophy and framework, the necessary structure and content of the preparation groups emerge. All of the following suggestions derive directly from comments by both categories of respondents.

- The daunting, undermining nature of the groups, so easily underestimated by project workers, so frequently alluded to by participants, can be lessened and transformed if the power of evaluation and assessment is, as much as possible, handed back to participants. In a paper on 'Preparing Families in Groups', O'Hara (1988) notes that a barrier to learning is 'a preoccupation with being accepted' (1988: 43). For too long, prospective adoptive parents have been made to grapple with this double bind.
- The numbers in any one series of groups should remain at an optimum

for experiential learning, from eight to ten. The pace should be dictated by the needs of the group, with plenty of informal and relaxation opportunities.

- Experienced adoptive parents should be invited to share equally in the planning and leading of some groups.
- 'Too much preparation too soon' may be a waste of everyone's time. The capacity for absorbing information and relating it to personal experience increases as confidence grows. Many respondents stated that there should be more specific training and preparation later in the process, continuing after placement. Some of this already happens in the project, with more planned.
- Too much emphasis on the difficulties is unbalanced and unhelpful. Positive case examples are also very important:

    B: 'We would have liked more case histories both successful and less successful plus discussion about them.'

- As much as possible, a balance of participants – with children, childless, black, single, etc. – should be achieved. In this study of white couples, a perceived bias against the minority group of childless participants was revealed, a bias that would have been felt even more acutely by members of other minority groups had they been represented. Yet childless couples, the minority group in question in this case, are very successful adoptive parents. Indeed the study by Borland *et al.* (1989: 57) suggests that childless adoptive parents achieve a higher 'success rate' with children aged ten and younger, than do adoptive parents who have birth children.

The comment of one respondent serves as a summary and slogan for this study:

'You could still be a good adoptive parent without attending the groups.'

Keeping this in mind should enable us to ensure that the preparation groups do not deter applicants who might otherwise become successful adoptive parents.

References

Borland, M., O'Hara, G. and Triseliotis, J. (1989) *Permanency Planning for Children in Lothian Region.* Edinburgh: University of Edinburgh.

Horne, J. (1983) Groupwork with prospective adopters, in Sawbridge, P. (ed.) *Parents for Children.* London: BAAF.

Kirk, D. (1964) *Shared Fate.* London: Collier-Macmillan.

Macaskill, C. (1985) *Against the Odds: Adopting Mentally Handicapped Children.* London: BAAF.

Nelson, K. (1985) *On the Frontier of Adoption: A Study of Special Needs Adoptive Families*. Washington: Child Welfare League of America.

O'Hara, G. (1988) Preparing families in groups, in Triseliotis, J. (ed.) *Groupwork in Adoption and Foster Care*. London: Batsford.

Ryburn, M. (1991) The myth of assessment, *Adoption and Fostering*, 15: 20–7.

Smith, C. (1988) Groupwork with prospective foster and adoptive parents, in Triseliotis, J. (ed.) *Groupwork in Adoption and Foster Care*. London: Batsford.

Stevenson, P. (1991) A model of self assessment for prospective adopters, *Adoption and Fostering*, 15: 30–4.

Thoburn, J. (1990) *Success and Failure in Permanent Family Placement*. Aldershot: Avebury.

Thoburn, J. and Rowe, J. (1988) A snapshot of permanent family placement, *Adoption and Fostering*, 12: 29–34.

Triseliotis, J. (1988) Introduction to the preparation and selection of adoptive and foster parents, in Triseliotis, J. (ed.) *Groupwork in Adoption and Foster Care*. London: Batsford.

Chapter 9

Increasing choice? The evaluation of Linburn Road Respite Care Unit, Dunfermline

Cameron MacVicar
Aberlour Child Care Trust

Introduction: objectives and methods

Twenty-one Linburn Road, Dunfermline, is a small residential respite care unit for families with children who have learning difficulties. It caters for children and young people up to 18 years old in the Dunfermline District. The service, a joint venture between Aberlour Child Care Trust and Fife Regional Council, was opened in March 1990. The unit was set up as a pilot project for two years. The purpose of the study was to evaluate whether the project was meeting the needs as outlined in the original proposal, to highlight areas of unmet need and to look at the quality of care being provided in the project.

This section sets out the objectives of the evaluation and the methods used, and looks at the background to the project, how it came to fruition and the first 15 months from March 1990 until June 1991. Further sections deal with an analysis of the data collected from interviews with parents and professionals, information from staff questionnaires and diaries, and finally the conclusions and recommendations.

The study attempted to address the following questions:

- Is the service meeting a perceived need as suggested in the original proposal?
- Is the service providing choice to parents?
- Is the unit offering a quality service?
- Is the service of value to those families using it?
- Is the project meeting the aims and objectives which have been set?

- Could the project offer more in terms of quality and time?
- Should the project continue?
- What would be the impact if the project terminated?
- Does the service complement other forms of respite care which are on offer in the area?

A qualitative approach was adopted. It was anticipated that this type of research would provide more depth and insight into the project. During the period of the research, 16 families were involved with the project, and with this relatively small number it was possible to carry out personal interviews with them all. This was also the case with the professionals who had contact with the project – again the numbers were relatively small.

Information was gathered using the following techniques:

- guided personal interviews with all parents using the service
- interviews with professionals who had referred or who had close contact with the unit
- observation by the staff team in respect of the work undertaken by them
- questionnaires completed by the staff team
- collection of data regarding use of the project.

The bulk of the time spent on the research was devoted to interviews with families. All the families who were using the project at the time agreed to be interviewed and they were seen at their homes. Written notes were taken during the interview and fully recorded afterwards.

To address the question of the quality of work being undertaken within the project, one of the methods used was observation by the staff team. This took the form of keeping a diary whilst on shift, and was undertaken by all staff (as outlined in Alaszewski and Oneg, 1990).

This abridged report of the study focuses on parents' experience of using the service and the quality of care offered by the unit as revealed by the diaries (see Appendix to this chapter). Views of staff and other professionals are more fully reported elsewhere (MacVicar, 1991).

Background

Aberlour Child Care Trust first became involved in the care of children with a mental handicap in 1985 when it opened a unit for eight children who had been discharged from Lynbank Hospital, a joint funding venture with Fife Regional Council Social Work Department and Fife Health Board.

The need for a respite care unit in Dunfermline District was indicated by a variety of sources. In 1985, The Scottish Child and Family Alliance were approached by a group of Fife parents and professionals and invited to run a counselling skills course in Fife for those involved with children with a mental handicap. As a result of the success of this course, further meetings were arranged through which a number of gaps in service provision within the region were identified, one of which was respite care. At this time, a group of parents with children with learning difficulties also identified a need for respite care.

In the light of this information Aberlour put forward a proposal in February 1989 to open a small residential respite service within Dunfermline District. The service was to cater for infants and youngsters aged up to 18 years and would operate from Friday lunchtime through to Sunday afternoon.

Referrals to the unit would be drawn from Dunfermline District. It was anticipated that referrals would be made by the Social Work Department, community health teams, hospitals and self-referrals from parents. Referrals would be assessed and placement offered accordingly. It was agreed there would be no charge made to parents for the use of the service. There were to be four part-time project workers with a part-time night-care worker, two relief project workers and one part-time secretary. Over and above this, it was anticipated there would be a number of volunteers involved in the unit.

The project opened on 9 March 1990. During the first 15 months, the project was open every weekend and four holiday periods: from March 1990 to June 1991, 20 youngsters had been accommodated in the unit.

During the initial period, demand for the project built up steadily. At first the unit was able to offer respite care on a four-week basis. However, it became evident that as demand grew this was not going to be possible. By the end of the summer of 1990 there were 15 youngsters receiving respite care. As a result of the demand, the project was able to offer respite only on a six-to-seven week cycle – a pattern which has remained.

The first six-monthly review of Linburn Road was held in August 1990. The major cause of concern for the staff team, supported by the parents, was the limited amount of time being offered by the project to families.

In October 1990, a paper was compiled outlining the need for an extension of the service. This proposal was for the project to be open from Friday through to Monday, with additional services being provided during the week. Unfortunately, Fife Region were unable to meet the costs of the additional resources. Aberlour Child Care Trust, however, did agree to the additional funding for the extension of the service for the second year of the pilot from April 1991 until March 1992. The additional service took the form of the project being open for one additional evening, that being Sunday and for an additional week during the summer holiday period.

From March until June 1991, the project admitted one other youngster, bringing the total number receiving respite to 16. It was the opinion of those managing the unit that 16 was the optimum number that could be accommodated. Any increase would result in the unit being unable to offer respite on a six-to-seven week cycle.

Data collection and analysis

The children and young people

The children and young people attending the project during the first 15 months had varying degrees of learning difficulties with a number having attendant physical disabilities. Three of the children required wheelchairs, whilst another five required to be in a 'buggy' when out of the home. Six of the children were doubly incontinent with another five requiring to wear nappies at night. The majority of the children could feed themselves to a certain extent; however, nine required some assistance with feeding. The sleep patterns of the children varied: eight slept well whilst the others were awake very early with one awake all night on occasions. However, staff indicated that their sleep patterns improved during the first 15 months. All children, apart from two, had little or no ability to play on their own and therefore required constant stimulation. The behaviour of the children varied a great deal, six of them being very disturbed and exhibiting various forms of difficult behaviour. One of the youngsters was physically aggressive towards staff and other children. Three of the youngsters had good verbal communication with one having limited Makaton (sign language), the others had limited or no verbal communication. With regards to medical requirements, seven suffered from epilepsy which was controlled. Nine required medication whilst the remainder caused no concern.

The following case illustrations highlight the differing degrees of learning difficulties. Note, however, that all the names of children and young people in this report have been changed.

Case A

Elizabeth, aged 10, is very dependent. She spends most of her time in a wheelchair although she can walk with aid from behind. She requires a body corset, splints and special boots. She is doubly incontinent and wears nappies during the day and at night. She requires all aspects of her personal hygiene carried out for her, and to be dressed and put to bed. However, she appears a happy youngster and does not exhibit any behavioural problems. She enjoys being taken out or listening to her music as well as staff attention.

Case B
John, aged 6, who has been diagnosed as having 'happy puppet syndrome', is hyperactive and is never quiet for any length of time. He has very poor concentration and can be unruly. He has few words but uses sign language, i.e. Makaton, and he can be understood by his gestures. He is not completely toilet trained and requires a nappy at night. He is a very poor sleeper and will wake in the middle of the night and not return to bed, something which his parents find extremely demanding.

Case C
Susan, aged 7, has multiple handicaps: she is hydrocephalic and suffers from epilepsy. She is extremely difficult to feed and requires to be fed via a stomach tube if her intake falls below a certain level during the course of a day. She also has little or no communication. This youngster requires a great deal of physical care. However, despite her handicaps she enjoys going out for walks and trips on the bus. She appears to respond to staff attention.

Case D
Donald, aged 11, has not been diagnosed as having any particular disability, but shows somewhat autistic tendencies. He can wash, dress, feed and toilet himself and has reasonable verbal communication. This youngster's major problem is his behaviour; he can become extremely demanding and if he does not get his own way he will throw a temper tantrum and swear. His behaviour has to be dealt with firmly. Whilst he gets on well enough with other children he much prefers his own company and when he comes to the project he will always bring his own toy car collection, which he loves to play with. However, he does not care to share them with others. At home he is also extremely demanding and, unfortunately, his older brother finds it difficult to invite friends in because of his behaviour. Until Linburn Road opened, the parents did not have a holiday or a break as they had no relations in the area they could call on.

Case E
Adrian, aged 16, is a difficult and disturbed young man who is extremely aggressive towards staff and other children. He is extremely destructive and requires a great deal of supervision, shows no responsibility for himself or others and recognizes no dangers. As a result, he cannot be taken out to the shops or the park as he would likely damage himself. His only source of pleasure appears to be musical tapes, audio and video. Due to his difficult behaviour he has been suspended from school and the only other form of respite he receives is in hospital. It is likely that he will require to be placed in

a long-term residential unit. As a result of his behaviour, this young man has to be taken into the project either on his own or with one other youngster.

Parental interviews

The parental interviews were carried out between April and June 1991. All of the 16 parents who had a child at Linburn Road were interviewed. All interviews took place at the family home and were conducted by the author.

The interviews focused on:

- use of the service
- their expectations of the service
- the impact of respite on the family
- the quality of contact they had with the project
- how they felt their son/daughter viewed the project
- comparisons with other forms of respite care which they may have been receiving
- the future of the project.

Use of the Project and expectations

All the families interviewed were receiving respite care on average once in six to seven weeks. All families apart from one were taking advantage of the additional night and found it to be of great benefit to them.

Ten of the families interviewed had used the service since it opened, the other six having been referred at different times since March 1990. The parents had heard of the resource from a variety of different contacts, including social workers, community mental handicap teams and also directly from another respite care unit.

With regard to expectations of the unit prior to its opening, six of the parents felt strongly that these had not been fully realized. They had expected respite care on a more frequent basis and that the unit would be open full time. Eight of the families felt that their expectations had been realized, whilst two families did not express an opinion.

Without exception, all parents felt that the aims and objectives which had been set at the six-monthly review in March 1991 were being met, especially in terms of the service alleviating stress within the families and the project offering a safe and caring environment.

Impact of respite on the family

Of the families interviewed, there was only one where there were no other siblings. In the 15 families where there were siblings, only two indicated that the service made no great difference to other members of their family. The other 13 families indicated that there were many posi- tive benefits for the other siblings when their brother or sister was at Linburn Road.

'Alan has two brothers and a baby sister. They enjoy the break. It means that they get out and they are given more time by us. It feels as though it is respite for them. It gives them more free time and they can get away with more when Alan is at Linburn Road.'

'Thomas has one brother. He enjoys the breaks when Thomas is at Linburn Road. We can do things together as a family, go to football with his father, stock-car racing, or go to the pictures or swimming. He will look at the calendar to see when Thomas is going to be at Linburn Road so that he can plan the weekend, i.e. what he is going to watch at the pictures.'

Those families with young children indicated that they were able to give much more of their time to them on the weekends when respite care was on offer. They suggested that the demands placed on them by their child with a handicap was such that they had little or no time to give to other members of their family.

The second question in this section concerned the positive gains which the whole family had derived from their son or daughter being at Linburn Road. The overwhelming view of the families was that there had been numerous gains for them having used respite. These included going out and having a meal together as a family, visits to the cinema, shops and on holiday.

'We can go and do our shopping much more easily. We can go out as a family to buy new clothes and this is not fraught with difficul- ties. One example was going through to the Glasgow Barras [a market] and being able to do this in peace. It is much easier to go to Asda when Thomas is at Linburn Road. It makes life a lot easier.'

'I enjoy having a long lie on a Saturday morning.'

Another area which was enhanced was the families' social life, especially that of the parents. One couple suggested that they went out during the course of the weekend when their daughter was at Linburn Road and this was a special time for them. Another couple suggested that it was easier to have friends in for a meal, whereas before when they had friends round they had very little peace as their son was not one for going to bed early.

Those families who used the respite during holiday times suggested that this had been extremely valuable and some were able to get away and have a holiday themselves with their other children. This resulted in the families feeling much more relaxed with their batteries having been recharged, which in turn allowed them to give more of their time and energy to their son or daughter.

The majority of families found that other family members were very supportive in their decision to utilize the facilities being provided for their child/young person at the unit. Three families indicated that there had been some negative reaction, but this had lessened once they became aware of the service provided at Linburn Road.

The final question in this section was in respect of whether it would have made a difference to the family if they had not received respite care. Fifteen of the families indicated strongly that it would have made a substantial difference to them and their child if they had not received respite care. Only one family indicated that it would not have made any difference if they had not received respite at Linburn Road.

> 'John is extremely hyperactive and he needs more attention than is normal, as a result of the difficulties which he exhibits. He hardly sleeps and we could not survive without Linburn Road. We would have had to look at the possibility of residential care. It would have increased the stress on our marriage which it may not have been able to withstand.'

> 'We would have cracked up. Pressures would have built up, frustrations would have built up. Jane can be extremely demanding and it is difficult at times to know what is wrong with her. This creates a great deal of tension in the house. We would require to have been at the doctors on numerous occasions.'

> 'I feel like walking out of the house at times. Pressure builds up terribly. It would have been worse without it. I would have left the house by now. I can get very tired and crabbit and would have been at breaking point. I look forward very much to the respite care.'

It is evident that there would have been major difficulties for certain families if Linburn Road had not existed (Gregory and Hennessy Powell, 1985: 93–4).

Parental contact with the project

Of the 16 parents interviewed, 13 of them indicated very positive relationships with the staff team (Wagner Committee, 1988: 45). One parent had no contact, whilst another two had little contact which for one was due to the distance involved and the fact that she had to rely on public transport. She said, however, that she would wish more contact with the project. A number of the 13 parents who indicated a positive relationship with the staff team, looked on them as friends as well as carers who looked after their youngster.

'Very friendly. If they meet you up the town they will go for a coffee with you. Feel as if I have known them for ages.'

'They are very good and you do not have to worry when Ian is there. On the 'phone they are quite honest and will tell you if there is a problem. I can contact them at any time.'

All, without exception, felt that the staff worked very much as a team and were aware of the young person's needs.

'Staff are very aware of the needs of John with regard to his drugs. John is allergic to food colouring and they are always careful what they give him to eat.'

'They appear to plan the weekend together. They work together during the course of the weekend. There is good team work.'

The view was that they were kept well informed by the project leader of dates when there was a vacancy in the unit.

One of the main methods of ensuring good communication was the introduction of a home-to-unit diary which the parents could write up and hand over to staff when the youngster came to the project, and for the staff to make comments on the youngster's weekend and return to the parents.

Eleven parents used the dairy and they found it of benefit.

'The diary has kept me informed of what my daughter has been doing over the course of the weekend.'

Jim's parents, however, felt that it would be valuable to have more information contained in the diary.

'We find the unit diary valuable; however, it is a bit short of entries with regard to what Jim has done over the weekend. Would like if possible after shift for staff to put a sentence in as to what Jim had been up to.'

Another method of assisting with communication was a parents' meeting held on the first Thursday of each month. Although eight of the parents did not attend the parents' meeting for a number of reasons (work, having a smaller child, distance), they all expressed an interest in attending in the future, if at all possible.

Those who did attend found it to be of value.

'Yes, I enjoy the coffee morning; it is information sharing and supportive and new ideas come up from them. Also gives more of a chance to meet the night staff.'

'Yes, enjoy them. Time to share information and meeting the other parents. I feel relaxed. The feedback from other parents is useful. The feedback from staff is valuable and it allows you to meet other staff.'

All who attended the parents' meetings said they would like them to continue.

Parental view of their child whilst attending the unit

For four of the parents it was difficult for them to give an indication as to whether or not their son or daughter looked forward to coming to the project, because of the nature of the child's handicap. One parent indicated that her son did not enjoy coming to the project.

'Friday morning he is okay. He appears quite happy. However, when he starts to think about it he will start crying.'

The other 11 parents indicated that their son or daughter enjoyed coming to the project.

'He looks forward to going to the project in the car. He appears to know that he is going as he becomes excited when he is near. He will jump up and down and is quite happy, saying "cheerio".'

'Very much so. He will pack his bags for his weekend.'

On return from the weekend, the majority of parents said that there were no problems when their son or daughter returned home. Three, however, indicated that their child could be somewhat high and excitable and it took a few hours for this to subside. One mum indicated that her son was really tired when he returned home. As to whether their son or daughter enjoyed their stay at Linburn Road, again four of the parents had some difficulty in assessing this, given their child's condition. However, 11 parents stated that their child did enjoy their time at Linburn Road.

'She does enjoy the stay. Talks about the staff team, her room and her crayons.'

'Appears to enjoy it. Laughs and giggles a great deal. No sign that he does not enjoy being at Linburn Road. He is one that enjoys the company of other children.'

All parents indicated that they were very happy with the care being provided for their child.

'On balance it is what we had hoped would be provided for Ian. Staff are caring and warm, and are very interested in getting to know what Ian's likes and dislikes are. Ian appears comfortable with the staff team.'

'It is very much like being at home. It has been created to be as near as possible like his home. He gets out and about enough. No complaints at all. They are very thorough in that they wash his clothes, which is something they do not have to do. A very good standard of care is provided. We would be able to tell staff if things were not right. Will eat certain foods at Linburn which he does not at home.'

In terms of any change in the type of care being provided, the majority of parents felt that the care that was on offer at Linburn Road was what they were looking for, and it was not something that they would wish to see dramatically altered. One parent said that she would like the staff to have more training in the use of Makaton sign language so as to enable them to communicate better with their son, whilst another felt that it would be useful if her daughter could get out more.

One of the main benefits which the parents saw for their son or daughter was their socializing with other adults and children. A number suggested that the staff at Linburn Road were able to offer opportunities to their child which they were unable to offer given their own situation.

'Gives Allan the opportunity to meet a lot more people. Extends his social contacts. He enjoys the excitement of being away from home as well as the change of being with different people. Makes me a better mum, therefore, this helps Allan. Extends his horizon in that they can provide things in the project that is not always possible at home.'

One other positive gain was the experience of being away from home, which would help the older youngsters prepare for the next stage in their lives.

'Another experience. It helps my daughter meet new people, being away from home gives her other experiences which will help her move towards the next stage in her life. It is hoped that my daughter will eventually move to a group home and I am sure that the experience at Linburn Road will have helped.'

Linburn Road in comparison with other forms of respite

The views of parents were sought as to how they saw Linburn Road in relation to other forms of respite care within the District, and whether it was complementary to them.

The main provider of respite care within Dunfermline is the Scottish Society for Mental Handicap through their Lend-A-Hand Scheme, a family-based scheme which has been operating for a number of years, and offers respite to approximately 40 children. There is also a limited amount of respite provided by Lynbank Hospital, in the main for the more severely disabled young person who requires medical care. Some of the families used Linburn Road only, some also used Lend-A-Hand Scheme or the hospital, and one family used all three.

The first question in this section looked at whether any families had received respite prior to Linburn Road being opened. Four of the families had not previously received any form of respite care. Four had received respite in a hospital setting, with three of these also having had respite via Lend-A-Hand Scheme. The remaining eight had received respite only via Lend-A-Hand Scheme, only four continuing to use this service. The main reasons given by the parents for not continuing to use Lend-A-Hand were that the caring family had moved away or that the caring family could no longer manage the youngster, given his or her behaviour.

For those families using Linburn Road and Lend-A-Hand, there was a wide range of what was on offer in terms of the time which they have with the carer, from a weekly evening meal to a whole weekend once a month.

The parents liked Linburn Road because, as a staffed house, it is reliable. When a date has been fixed for the youngster to come in they know that they will have respite at that time. For those families who receive respite care in hospital as well as Linburn Road, their view was that Linburn Road was much more appropriate as there are fewer youngsters around and the staff ratio is much higher; their youngster received a great deal more attention and, therefore, increased stimulation.

Future use of the project

All parents, without exception, indicated that they would wish to see the service at Linburn Road developed further. What they would wish for was the project to be open on a full-time basis. For those parents with limited extended family nearby, they would very much value the unit being open full time to provide emergency cover.

Parents were asked if they would be interested in a sitting service; the majority indicated that they would, especially if this was provided by staff from Linburn Road.

'Would use it more often. Have no extended family nearby therefore have no baby-sitting. Cannot do things as much as we would like.'

'Would like one weekend per month. If it were open full time would use it for a breather during the week – possibly for a few hours after school.'

With regard to whether it would make a major difference in their lives if Linburn Road were to close, five of the families indicated that this would raise the question as to whether their youngster could remain at home.

'Does not bear thinking about. It would be a disaster for all concerned. Would perhaps require Andrew going into residential care.'

All the families were of the opinion that if Linburn Road was not available then there would be increased pressure on the whole family which would be detrimental.

The final question was with regard to whether suitable alternative respite would be available to the families. Those families who received Lend-A-Hand expressed the view that they would require more from that service. Of those who were not receiving Lend-A-Hand, four indicated that they would have to try the scheme. Three of these families had received Lend-A-Hand in the past, but it had not worked for them. Five other families indicated that they would have no alternatives. Three families indicated that as a last resort they would have to look at the possibility of using hospital respite care.

The care of children and young people

The care the clients receive was observed by the staff team during the course of a shift. Staff were given a diary sheet to complete, based on Alaszewski and Oneg (1990), with guidelines on the information which was to be recorded. This included times of arrivals, telephone calls, visits, outings and interaction with young people and between staff. They were also asked to give a description of the young people in the project during the course of the observation. Observations were carried out on three separate occasions during the course of two weekends and two days midweek during the Easter holidays.

The following illustrates work undertaken by staff during a shift at Linburn Road. There were three youngsters in the unit:

Ian
Ian is a three-and-a-half-year-old who is hemiplegic and has limited vision, as a result of a non-accidental injury. He requires assistance with feeding and drinking and is in nappies at all times. He is, however, mobile and can get around the house; he enjoys musical toys and videos and responds to staff affection, e.g. cuddles and kisses. [This was Ian's first weekend in the project.]

David
David is ten years of age and suffers from cri du chat syndrome. He cries and whines most of the time, which hinders communication with

him. David is quite bright and can do a good deal for himself if he wishes, such as dress, feed himself. He also has a fair degree of speech; however, when at Linburn Road he is inclined to cry most of time.

John
John is a six-year-old who suffers from 'happy puppet syndrome', described earlier. He came in on the Saturday.

Friday

12 noon	All staff on duty for staff meeting.
2.00 p.m.	Staff meeting completed. Staff leave apart from the two (Nicola and Christine) on duty for the remainder of the day. They prepare for children arriving.
3.00 p.m.	David arrives straight from school, is very unhappy. Ian arrives with mum. Christine discusses David's drugs with mum.
4.00 p.m.	Staff and children go into town and have a burger. Children enjoy outing.
6.00 p.m.	Arrive back at home. David starts crying, then soils himself and is changed by Nicola. Christine checks children's clothes and puts them away; fills in drugs book.
7.00 p.m.	Children given a drink. Ian watches 'Singing Kettle' [a children's folk group] video, quite happy with staff. David continues crying and then wets himself. Project leader arrives for a short time.
8.00–10.00 p.m.	David goes to bed. Ian changed and made ready for bed. Ian unhappy going to bed. Nicola and Christine spend time comforting him and staying in bedroom; does not settle; gets up. Christine puts on washing and tidies up the kitchen. Nicola, in between comforting Ian, tries to write-up log and do petty cash. David now sleeping. Ian still up on arrival of night staff (Shona).
10.00–12.00 p.m.	Ian requires a lot of reassurance. Shona has to cuddle him to get him to sleep – goes down at 11.45 p.m. Shona then checks David – sound asleep.
12.00 p.m.–2.00 a.m.	David's mum telephones to check how he is. Both boys sleeping soundly. Checked at regular intervals. Shona does ironing.
2.00–5.00 a.m.	Boys checked at regular intervals; all quiet.

5.00–6.30 a.m.	David awake at 5.00 a.m. – comes through to living room and watches television. Ian awake at 5.30 a.m., was upset, appears to be missing mum. Both boys bathed and dressed before day shift.

Day shift – Nicola and Christine

7.30–8.00 a.m.	Watch television with the boys and Shona given feedback on night shift.
8.00–9.00 a.m.	Children given a cooked breakfast. Staff assistance with feeding required. Christine tidies up kitchen. David starts crying.
9.00–10.00 a.m.	John arrives with parents. Nicola has a chat with them and a cup of tea. David continues to be very demanding.
10.00–11.00 a.m.	Staff play and to do some craft work with the children; they show little or no interest.
11.00 a.m.–1.00 p.m.	Children taken out for a walk. David quiet during walk – starts crying on return.
1.00–2.00 p.m.	Children given lunch, assisted by staff.
2.00–2.30 p.m.	Backshift arrive – hand over of information takes place. David continues to be very difficult, continues crying. John very active and requiring a good deal of attention. Ian seeking reassurance from staff as this is his first weekend.

From the observation sheets, it was very evident that all the children and young people have varying needs. When the project was initially set up, it was envisaged that many children would be matched, compatible groups would emerge and they would come in to the unit together. Because of the differences between the children, this has not happened as had been anticipated.

The staff: child ratio at Linburn Road allows for a good deal of individual contact with the children and young people, and a degree of flexibility. Linburn Road aims to provide children and young people with a high level of stimulation. At times it is possible for staff to go out with one child. This is important for the child who does not receive a great deal of individual attention at home. Given that there are two members of staff on duty at all times during the day, it is possible to take the children on outings to the park, beach, fun fair, safari park, etc., especially during holiday periods. One problem that the staff encounter is the lack of transport at times, as not all staff drive. However, they do have the use of Bellyeoman Road's minibus which is of great value.

In the course of a weekend or holidays, staff will do things at the pace of the children. Whilst the unit has structures in terms of staff shifts, there is a good deal of flexibility within that. The children and young people get up when they want to, the older ones if they so wish can lie in on a Saturday or Sunday. They do not have to be up in time for the morning shift coming in. Linburn's bedtimes are adjusted to the needs and wishes of the children and young people.

Staff at Linburn Road require a great deal of physical and emotional energy, given the demands of the young people. It is very evident from observing staff and feedback from parents that they have a great deal of compassion, understanding and love for the children that they are caring for. This results in a standard of care which they are committed to.

Effects on the client

In the context of respite care the primary client is somewhat difficult to determine. Whilst it is the young person who is being physically cared for, the needs of the parents are of equal importance as they are the ones who require the respite to enable them to continue the care of their child. The way in which the facility allows this to happen was evident from the interviews undertaken with the parents. The service being provided by Linburn Road seems to have had a very positive effect on the majority of the parents.

The effect on the children is somewhat more difficult to gauge, given that the children are only in the unit for short periods of time and there are large gaps in time between visits (six to seven weeks). Accounts of staff suggest that the sleep patterns of those youngsters with disturbed sleep improved. They are of the view that the behaviour of certain youngsters improved and the youngsters who were more insular are now inclined to take part in activities. It is difficult to judge whether this would have happened naturally, given the children are older, or whether it was part of the settling-down process, with the children feeling more comfortable in the project.

One of the frustrations of the staff team is that children do not come to the project more often. It is their opinion that if this was the case then they would be able to assist in bringing about positive changes, especially with those children who are on special programmes from school.

Conclusions

Linburn Road was set up to provide good quality respite care in a small residential facility for those families who had indicated a desire for an increase in the choice of respite care for their child. The evaluation has attempted to look at whether this was achieved during its first year of operation.

Is the service meeting the perceived need as suggested in the original proposal?

During the first 15 months of operation, 20 families had used Linburn Road. At the end of June 1991, 16 families were using the service on a regular basis. With the service being part time, families were receiving respite on average every seven weeks for a weekend. The information from the parents indicated that their needs were not being met in full as a result of the part-time nature of the project. This view was also expressed by a number of professionals. One of the main needs not being met was for emergency accommodation.

Is the service providing choice to parents?

One of the main aims of the project was to offer choice to parents with regard to the form of respite care which they wished for their son or daughter. Parents have exercised this choice: there are families who use Linburn Road as opposed to other forms of respite care on offer in the area.

Is the unit offering a quality service?

The general view of parents and professionals was that the service is of a high standard. Parents indicated that they were happy and confident in the staff team and that their child was well looked after at Linburn Road.

Is the service of value to those families using it?

The overwhelming view was that both parents and other siblings in the families benefited greatly when their child was at Linburn Road. It enabled them to relax and enjoy time with their other children. This in turn made them more able to cope with their child on return from Linburn Road.

Is the project meeting the aims and objectives which have been set?

All those interviewed are of the opinion that the project was meeting the declared aims and objectives.

Could the project offer more in terms of quality and time?

The majority view was that the project was limited in the service that it could offer, given that it was only open on a part-time basis. From the evaluation, it is evident that a great deal more could be offered by the project if it were open full time. One of the main drawbacks of the project was the fact that it lacked flexibility and could not always offer the respite when the parents required it.

Should the project continue?

All those who took part in the evaluation were strongly of the opinion that the project should continue and should be expanded to a full-time service.

What would be the impact if the project terminated?

If the project were to terminate at the end of the pilot period, the majority of parents indicated that it would create major difficulties for them in that it would take away choice, and for some it would result in having to ask the hospital to provide them with respite. Five of the families indicated that they would have great difficulty in sustaining their youngster at home and might have to consider residential care.

Does the service complement other forms of respite care which are on offer in the area?

Linburn Road has established itself as one of the main providers of respite care in Dunfermline. It provides choice and additional respite to certain families. It does appear to complement other forms of respite care.

Recommendations

- Linburn Road should continue as a respite facility following the completion of the pilot period in March 1992.
- Linburn Road should, in the future, open on a full-time basis so as to offer more flexibility in its service provision.
- Similar resources to Linburn Road should be established in other locations, to be one of a range of respite resources to those parents who are wishing an element of choice for their child.

Postscript

The evaluation of Linburn Road was primarily carried out to look at whether there was a continuing need for a small residential respite facility within Dunfermline District. From the research, it was evident that there was a need, that the type of service being provided should be increased and that similar resources should be available elsewhere.

The evaluation was a useful tool in securing the long-term future of the project, as it clearly evidenced that the unit was meeting an identifiable need. As a result, Linburn Road has continued to offer weekend and holiday respite care and is at the time of writing in its fifth year of operation. Numbers using the project have increased, and there are now 20 children/young people who receive respite care on a regular basis. The demand for the service has grown during the past two years and there are presently ten families on the waiting list. It was decided by the unit that if they were to offer respite to more than 20 children/young people, the service being delivered would be so diluted that it would be of limited value.

As a result of the evaluation, and the ever-increasing demand for respite care, Aberlour Child Care Trust put forward two proposals to Fife Region Social Work Department towards the end of 1992. One was to develop Linburn Road into a full-time resource; the second, to develop a similar project to Linburn Road in the East of Fife. Unfortunately, owing to lack of funding at that time, it was not possible to proceed. However, the Regional Council's Social Work Department in their Community Care Plan 1992–95 were committed to the development of another small residential respite facility in the East of Fife. This was again the case in their 1994–97 Community Care Plan which was published during 1993. Towards the end of 1993, Fife Region put out to tender the management of a weekend residential respite care facility in the East of Fife. Aberlour Child Care Trust tendered for this piece of work, and included in the tender document a summary of the evaluation of Linburn Road. Aberlour's tender was accepted and they have now entered into a contract to provide this service, in the first instance for a three-year period.

The evaluation of Linburn Road has made a positive contribution to Aberlour's continued development in the field of residential respite care. The organization has built up a degree of expertise in this area of work and has been invited to put forward proposals for respite care in other areas of Scotland. It is going to be important to continue to develop services as it is evident that the need for respite care, whether it be residential or family-based, has increased during the last ten years. This is likely to continue to be the trend for the foreseeable future, given that more children and young people with learning disabilities are being cared for in the community.

References

Alaszewski, A. and Oneg, B.N. (1990) *Normalization in Practice*. London: Routledge and Kegan Paul.

Gregory, S. and Hennessy Powell, T. (1985) Community-based respite care, *Mental Handicap*, 13: 93–4.
Wagner Committee (1988) *Residential Care: A Positive Choice*. London: HMSO.

Appendix

Diary used by staff

Guidelines for staff diaries

- Factual information, e.g. what has happened, arrival, telephone calls, visits, outings.
- Interaction with young people.
- Interaction between staff.
- Qualitative aspects of the work being carried out, i.e. How does it feel, good, bad or indifferent?
- Description of young people in the project.

Sample diary format

Day Shift	Night Shift
Friday, 12 p.m.	Friday, 10 p.m.
Friday, 3 p.m.	Friday, 11 p.m.
Friday, 5 p.m.	Saturday, 1 a.m.
Friday, 6 p.m.	Saturday, 3 a.m.
Friday, 7 p.m.	Saturday, 5 a.m.
Friday, 8 p.m.	Saturday, 7 a.m.
Friday, 9 p.m.	Saturday, 8 a.m.
Friday, 10 p.m.	

Chapter 10

Parents of children with cancer: their perceptions of social work help

Jean M. Smith
Royal Hospital for Sick Children, Edinburgh

Introduction

Families of children who are diagnosed as having cancer are confronted by a crisis which may affect all aspects of their lives. They commonly have to face a wide variety of difficulties such as supporting their child undergoing tests and treatment, managing other children at home, dealing with practical arrangements and employment and, above all, coping with anxiety, uncertainty, fear and loss created by the illness. The social work approach is to offer help with practical, emotional and social aspects of the illness. The establishment of a good relationship between the social worker and the family is regarded by many practitioners as an important element in the treatment and an important factor in determining whether the child can get the maximum help from medical treatment.

The purpose of this small study was to examine some of the factors which contribute to the crisis parents face when their child is first diagnosed as possibly having cancer or leukaemia, in particular to seek parents' views of the contact they had with the social worker and identify aspects which were considered to be either helpful or unhelpful. It was hoped that the results would have lessons for practice in that they would suggest ways in which the social work service could be made more accessible to families.

The research, therefore, focused on obtaining parents' views on the following questions:

- What problems do families face at the onset of the child's illness?
- How do they react to being referred to a social worker?
- Did they value the social work help they received?
- In what ways was that service helpful or unhelpful and how can improvements be made?

Method and context of study

The study was undertaken at the Royal Hospital for Sick Children, Edinburgh, in 1991. The Oncology Unit is a regional treatment centre for all of the South East of Scotland, providing treatment each year for about 35 children who are newly diagnosed, as well as ongoing care and follow-up treatment for the others. The treatment team at the time of the study was headed by a consultant paediatric haematologist/oncologist and the team was multidisciplinary. The Malcolm Sargent Cancer Fund for Children provided funds for two part-time social work posts to enable the provision of a specialist social work service for all the families who attend the unit.

The sample were the parents of a cohort of children who were diagnosed in 1990–91 as having leukaemia or cancer. Excluded from the study were families who had moved away from the area and families of children who had died. This left a total of 19 families. Of these, two were unwilling to participate and in another family the child had died before the parents were due to be interviewed. This left a sample of 16 families. In-depth semistructured interviews were conducted with both parents where practicable, but in some instances only one parent, usually the mother, was seen. Families were interviewed for the study, on average, 10 months after they had first come to the hospital.

The families were approached initially by letter which informed them about the research study and asked for their help and participation. It provided an opportunity for them to refuse to take part by returning a tear-off slip. None of the families returned this. The letter was followed by a telephone call to arrange a date for an interview. It was decided to interview all the families at home as it was felt parents would be more relaxed and able to give more considered replies. One parent was interviewed in the hospital ward because of her child's extended hospitalization.

The schedule was designed to look, *inter alia*, at the following areas:

- the degree and type of contacts with the social worker
- circumstances of referral
- attitudes to social work in general
- perceptions of helpfulness and unhelpfulness of social work in their particular experience

- parents' suggestions for ways of improving the way social work service is offered
- parents' perceptions of the problems they faced as a result of the child's illness.

The families in the sample represented for the most part cases held by the researcher and by her colleague in the Oncology Unit with three families being cases held by social work students under supervision, and one a case held by another social worker in the department. It was recognized that there could be some differences in response between the responses of the researcher's own clients and those of others. The researcher acknowledged in the interviews the respondents might have more inhibitions about frank responses in this situation, especially where possible negative answers were sought. In practice, there seemed to be no difficulties in this respect, and there was no evidence of differences in response between those of the researcher's own clients and those of others.

The families

The families came from across the range of socio-economic groups and were largely two-parent families with an average 2.25 children. There were lone single-parent families comprising unemployed, single mothers. In the two-parent families, eight of the fathers had skilled manual work, two had unskilled or semiskilled work, two owned their own businesses and two were employed in the professions. Only three of the families had previous contact with social workers, two of them on a minimal basis for reasons connected with work rather than their family circumstances while one parent had been in care in her own childhood, an experience which had biased her against social work.

Reaction to the diagnosis

All 16 families indicated that the diagnosis had come as a complete shock. Most also feared that their child would die. Ten of the families said that when they brought their child to the hospital they knew the illness would be a serious one, while six admitted that they had underestimated the medical situation. Four of this latter group and ten families in all had no idea that treatments were available for children with cancer.

The parents were asked about the people to whom they had turned for help. Twelve of the families responded that the spouse was the important person. Other people who were said to have been supportive at first were the following: the extended family, friends, health professionals,

Figure 10.1   Incidence of problems reported by families (*n* = 15).

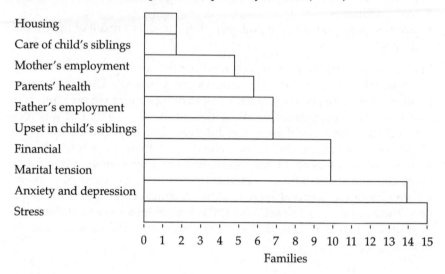

clergy and other parents of children with cancer. No-one felt completely unsupported. Everyone interviewed was given a list of possible problems they might have had to face and asked to indicate those which had produced a major effect on themselves. Responses are indicated in Figure 10.1.

If the categories 'stress', feelings of 'anxiety and depression', 'marital tension' and 'upset in child's siblings' are regarded as being mainly of an emotional nature and the remaining ones as basically 'practical', the high preponderance of emotional difficulties in the responses seems significant. Some further clues to the degree of distress of many of the parents can be seen in additional comments which included the following:

'He [the child] was angry and this was directed at me.'

'It sorted out who were your real friends.'

'Both she and I missed the other children at home when we were in hospital and felt isolated.'

'I see other children running about uncared for and it makes me feel angry.'

'It affected all the family. My nephews thought they were going to get cancer too.'

Seeing the social worker

As part of the assessment process, all the families attending the unit either on an in-patient or out-patient basis meet with the social worker

Table 10.1 Families' initial reactions to seeing a social worker ($n = 16$).

Very positive	0
Positive	1
Neutral	1
Negative	9
Antagonistic	5

irrespective of their circumstances or apparent need. The purpose of the social work assessment is to identify any difficulties the family are facing and where appropriate, offer and arrange to help. All the families in the study were asked about their initial reaction to being told that they were expected to see a social worker.

The responses of the families were noted and grouped in five categories producing the results shown in Table 10.1.

The one positive comment was 'I thought I would need help' and the neutral reaction was 'It didn't strike us as odd but we didn't need help'. Examples of negative and antagonistic comments included the following:

'What could she possibly do to help?'

'I was taken aback at the idea.'

'It seemed irrelevant.'

'What have I done, is it my fault?'

'I felt like saying "Go away".'

'Oh no, she'll be in our lives all the time.'

When asked to amplify some of their comments by describing what they thought social workers did, several of the parents revealed some of the fears which lay behind their attitudes. Social workers were regarded as being concerned about child abuse, problem families and financial difficulties, as well as 'taking your bairns away' and 'part of the banner-waving loony Left'. By way of balance, it should be noted also that many of the research interviews were conducted at the time when much media attention was focused on the 'pin-down' abuse of children occurring in the children's homes in Staffordshire. A few of the parents were able to say that they had been afraid that a referral to the social worker was due to the hospital staff's belief that they had contributed to the causation of the child's illness.

Perceptions of helpfulness and unhelpfulness of their social work contact

Parents were shown two separate lists of some general social work features (as shown in Tables 10.2 and 10.3), and asked to identify those

Table 10.2 Families' perceptions of 'helpfulness' ($n = 16$).

The Social Worker	
Is someone to talk to in confidence	14
Will listen	13
Can provide information	11
Isn't surprised or upset at what you say	11
Can provide financial help	10
Is someone to talk to outside the family	7
Can help with practical arrangements	5
Can be a link with medical and nursing staff	3
Is someone to talk to away from your child	2
Can arrange special things for the child	2
Can help to change the child's behaviour	2
Other (person unable to list any of these)	1

which they considered to be the most important. They were then asked to draw on their own recent experience of social work and identify aspects which had been particularly helpful for them and (as it seemed unlikely that many would say outright what had been unhelpful) asked to indicate aspects that could have been more helpful to them.

The responses shown in Table 10.2 emphasize the high value parents attached to having someone to talk to in confidence outside of the family. It was apparent also that the notion that talking constructively about their problem would be helpful in itself was a novel one to many parents. Some of the comments illustrate these points more clearly:

- 'I had not thought of talking about things before and it helped.'
- 'It was important to have someone not caught up in the worries; someone outside the family.'
- 'You can put on a show for your friends but you [social workers] know it is not like that.'
- 'You can't talk about fears of her dying to your friends and family.'
- 'Saying things out loud brings the reality home.'
- 'It was important to discuss with a social worker what would happen later.'

It is interesting to note that whilst the parents marked a total of 81 characteristics on the 'helpful' list as being relevant to their situation they only identified 35 characteristics of 'unhelpfulness'. As Table 10.3 shows, less than half of the parent sample identified any negative features and some parents identified very few indeed. The one characteristic, from a list expressing feelings about social work, which attracted an agreement from more than half the sample was 'The social worker is yet another

Table 10.3 Families' perceptions of 'unhelpfulness' (*n* = 16).

The Social Worker	
Is yet another person to see	9
Makes others think you can't cope	6
Makes you feel uncomfortable	5
Asks too many questions	4
Has no idea what parents are going through	3
Had not enough medical knowledge	3
Had no children of his/her own	2
May be critical	2
Is too young or too old	1

Table 10.4 Receipt of practical help and families' views of the importance of social workers (*n* = 15).

	Received practical help	*Did not receive practical help*
Contact with social worker important or very important	7	0
Contact with social worker fairly important or unimportant	4	4

person to see'. This suggested a more general irritation with the many intensive procedures required by hospitalization. Apart from two, families were largely uncritical of the social work service they received. Some were able to make suggestions about the way social workers should approach parents.

The value of social work

An attempt was made in the study to see if there was any correlation between the importance individual families attached to their contact with social workers and the type of help they had received. It is relevant here to note when the families had indicated practical problems during the diagnostic process the social workers were usually able to help, in some cases drawing on financial help from the Malcolm Sargent Cancer Fund which can be used for a variety of purposes and is easily accessible. The analysis showed (see Table 10.4) that families who rated social work 'important' or 'very important' had received practical kinds of help

Figure 10.2   Rating of changes in attitudes to social work. Shaded areas show degree of attitude change.

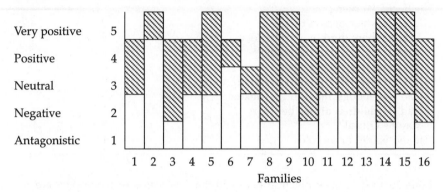

whereas those who rated social work as 'fairly important' or 'unimportant' had not had many practical problems and had received little practical help.

Another way in which the value of the social work was measured was by comparing each family's self-reported predisposition to seeing a social worker with their level of satisfaction at the social work service they received. One reason for doing this was that there seemed to be a discrepancy between the importance of social work as rated by parents and opinions being expressed by parents in other parts of the interview. This measurement was a more complex one as it involved the researcher in rating the responses to four separate questions to give a measure of the level of client satisfaction. The researcher's own rating was checked independently to ensure a degree of objectivity. The results shown in Figure 10.2 are interesting. In every case, the 'client satisfaction' rating was higher than that of the initial responses to seeing a social worker. While it would be wrong to draw any general conclusions from such a small sample, as well as from this particular type of practitioner research, it can be noted that some of the changes in attitude to social work are quite significant.

Improving social work service

No consistent theme emerged in the families' suggestions on ways in which service could be improved, apart from the almost unanimous view that social workers should always see both parents whenever this is possible.

Questions about usefulness of groups as a mechanism for offering

Table 10.5 Families' preferences on timing of first contact with social workers (*n* = 16).

As soon as possible	2
Within a week	9
It does not matter	1
After a period longer than one week	4

mutual support especially when children were receiving treatment produced inconclusive results. Nine families saw benefit in meeting with other families of children with cancer in this way, while the remainder held the contrary view. Another specific matter about which families' views were sought concerned the point in the assessment and diagnostic procedures at which parents and social workers should first meet. The preferences are shown in Table 10.5.

Eleven families commented that they did not think it was helpful to see the social worker too soon because the immediate concern was for the health of the child; they saw the focus on the medical diagnosis and clinical treatment as being uppermost in the initial stages and wanted the social work contact to come after this period. However, it was interesting to note that in suggesting a delay nine of the families still wanted the meeting to take place within a week.

Discussion

A useful purpose of practitioner research is that it can provide objective evaluation of an aspect of service and so make a contribution to an agency's own examination of the quality of its work. In as much as it systematically heard and noted parents' views and, subsequently, enabled their viewpoint to have an influence on the agency's review of its procedures, this study achieved its primary objective. While it would be inappropriate to make any generalizations from such a small sample, there were several aspects which merit discussion and point to areas which could be followed up in further research. Peace *et al.* (1991) have pointed out in a recent overview of the literature on childhood cancer that 'there are significant gaps in our knowledge in aspects of individual coping, the family as a unit and the family within its social and cultural environment'.

The study highlighted the family's unpreparedness for the diagnosis in their child, the lack of knowledge of treatment and the possible medical implications of cancer. It also showed the large number of problems the families felt they faced at the time of the onset of the illness and in particular the prevalence of emotional difficulties. The fact that the parents in this study were more inclined to assess their contact with a social worker as being important if they had received practical help (for example, financial assistance with the costs of travelling) should not necessarily be seen as an indication that help with their emotional difficulties was not forthcoming. There is good evidence from their responses that they valued talking with a social worker although they were unwilling to describe this experience as 'help'. This finding is consistent with the research by Mayer and Timms (1970) which showed that clients are less inclined to acknowledge having been helped with emotional difficulties.

The very negative predisposing views about social work and the subsequent changes in attitude have been discussed above. One clear implication for hospital practices is that the referral to the social worker should be handled sensitively by the doctor, nurse or receptionist. A clear explanation of the purpose of the contact is necessary. Subsequently, the social worker should take time in the first interview to explore any negative or ambivalent feelings and be able to provide clear and convincing explanations as to why social work help is being offered to the family.

For many families in this study, their contacts with social work services were still very much at an early stage. Many of the children will require regular visits to the hospital, and possibly in-patient treatment for years to come. These children and their parents are trying to cope with a life-threatening illness and there may well be further crises to come. From this study, one can have some grounds for hoping that if the child relapses and the illness returns, the parents would be able to turn more readily to the social workers for support in the future.

References

Mayer, J.E. and Timms, N. (1970) *The Client Speaks*. London: Routledge and Kegan Paul.

Peace, G., O'Keeffe, C., Faulkner, A. and Clark, J. (1991) Childhood cancer: psychosocial needs. Are they being met?, *Journal of Cancer Care*, 1: 3–13.

Part Four

Afterword, Appendices and Bibliography

Chapter 11

Afterword: Towards more reflexive practice?

Does practitioner research in social work live up to its promise as (to echo the statement with which we opened this book) an idea whose time has come? It is one thing to show that, given the tools, practitioners can carry out research, another to demonstrate that it constitutes a serious addition to their professional development, and yet another to show that the larger canvas of research on social work practice is significantly enhanced by a cadre of research-active and research-minded practitioners.

The focus of the book has been on helping practitioners to get to grips with a serious research enquiry, carry it out, and do something with the results. Two things are immediately apparent from our own experience of working with practitioner–researchers. To us as professional researchers, the enthusiasm and commitment of the various groups which have passed through the Stirling programme have been impressive. And we have been struck no less by the enjoyment that they seem to have derived from tackling the problems and (in the way of all research) partially resolving them. But what of the end product? There are several questions here which demand reflection.

The intrinsic value of the research

Does the choice of topic open up new or unfamiliar lines of enquiry? Do the methods that they use focus appropriately on what skills the researchers have already as practitioners, or are they disappointingly constrained by them? Can practitioners overcome difficulties stemming from their lack of experience and their putative insider bias, and produce results of reasonable 'rigour'? The extracts in Part Three will have given readers an opportunity to assess this, and we return later in this chapter to a consideration of the quality of the research produced.

Impact on agency practice

The gap between research and 'implementation' is well known in social policy research. There are many reasons for widespread failure to act on research findings, including the gulf which inevitably exists between empirical work and questions of what should be done. One factor commonly at work, however, is the remoteness of external researchers from the agency context. Can practitioners overcome some at least of the barriers which may obstruct the reception of research findings? Does their role within the service delivery agency result in findings being taken more seriously or seen more credibly, in their implications for management or practice being discussed with more good faith, in changes being pushed through and monitored with greater commitment?

The wider development of research-mindedness

Beyond the issue of how an individual piece of work may be received, does the experience for colleagues of having a researcher in their midst leave any residue of increased recognition of the scope (and limitations) of research, of greater receptivity to research more generally, of an impulse to ask for the evidence when policy or managerial pronouncements are made? For agency managers, does the experience of observing the trials and triumphs of the eventual emergence of research findings leave them with a more sympathetic attitude towards research, an eagerness to consult research when changes are planned, or a greater capacity to build research, monitoring or evaluation into the implementation of change? In other words, do research activities of the kind described help to create and nurture a research culture in the agencies?

Professional development

Social workers are enjoined to acquire research skills as part of their professional repertoire, and there is no doubt that the demonstration of a completed research study looks impressive on a CV. But do they become better social workers as a result of their research? In what ways, precisely, does the research perspective translate into improved performance as professional social workers or managers?

The practitioners' viewpoint

These are searching questions, and constitute demanding tests for practitioner research. Any account of the success of the venture must be tempered not only by an awareness of what might reasonably be expected, but also by the consideration that the process of learning something about research by doing it may be as important as the end product.

Some of these questions are unanswerable, but tentative responses to others are available from results of follow-up questionnaires sent to participants in the first two years of the practitioner-research programme (PRP). First, however, it is evident, as from all the feedback that we have received, that participants found the programme a professionally significant and personally enjoyable experience. All of the following general comments offer interesting perspectives on what it is like to do practitioner research, and by implication about what reflection it casts on routine social work practice.

'I found the "sacred" time at the university was very refreshing. It was also stimulating and morale-boosting to feel special.'

'The PRP was a very valuable experience for me and one that I would like to build on in small as well as larger ways. My project hopes to undertake research into other areas . . . we have participated in allied research.'

'PRP was a very stimulating experience at a time in my life when I was looking for some direction. I am sure it had a direct influence on me gaining my present post . . .'

'The whole PRP experience was a good one for me and my agency. I would like to do it again and do it even better. The PRP may be the only way I could focus on a thorough piece of research again.'

'PRP gave me self-confidence – research was possible for ordinary practitioners and not something "out there" for people in ivory towers.'

'Without this opportunity a struggling voluntary agency could not have undertaken the work . . . [Funders] just assume that we can take on monitoring work.'

'[Research] is addictive.'

'[I] found the experience challenging but having gained knowledge and skills would welcome some opportunity to use these.'

'I feel more confident about passing comment on a piece of research and also assisting others to understand the basics.'

'The PRP:
    gives status to practitioners by recognizing the importance of
    issues *they* face;'

... facilitates production of a high-quality (and esteemed) piece of work;'

... is time-limited, so however hard it may seem at the time you know at the end you will have produced something;'

... has a very beneficial influence on the rest of my work;'

... facilitates production of many extremely interesting and diverse topics which otherwise would not have come to light because they would not attract management funding.'

'I enjoyed the experience so much that I've applied and been accepted to do a MPhil or PhD.'

'I was inspired by your programme and the faith you had in the participants. People do respond to high expectations and clear timescales.'

Providing agreeable and professionally fulfilling 'time out' for practitioners is not to be discounted. Expectations may, however, be couched in the higher aspirations implied by the questions with which this chapter opened.

Evidence of impact on the practitioner's host agency is, inevitably, elusive and uncertain. A small number only felt able to make the confident claim of this respondent:

'My research, combined with other developments, is being used to restructure the whole of the assessment and training process.'

While only two respondents reported a major impact on practice or policy, however, only two reported 'little or no' impact. The majority saw smaller or less dramatic changes to practice or policy having come about as a result of their research, usually in their own practice or that of their team, while a significant minority reported that if effects on practice were difficult to detect, the findings of the study had at least made people think about their activities. A number had evidently learned that 'the impact of research is likely to be a slow process' and commented (some eight months after the event) that it was too early to say what was likely to happen as a result.

It was not only in the fate of substantive findings, however, that the effects of practitioner research were identified; there were less tangible outcomes. A common theme was that the influence on colleagues of participation in research itself had led to changed attitudes to research:

'It has made people aware that research can be useful and relatively user-friendly.'

'The practitioners involved in the study and others who heard of it recognized the need to monitor practice.'

'The agency has benefited mostly through a heightened awareness of research . . . It encourages others to take account of research and perhaps to participate in it. It also enables the team to be presented as one in which research has a part to play.'

Examples were given of instruments designed for the practitioner's study being retained and built permanently into a periodic process of monitoring and review. While these suggest a positive influence of the kind hoped for, other respondents pinpointed difficulties in promulgating a research culture:

'The successful application [for admission to] the programme was made much of, but the findings and recommendations were basically ignored . . . I wonder if managers actually need to learn how to use research.'

and

'The agency would have benefited more if, having sent us on the PRP, it had carried [this] through by demanding the results as part of the department's knowledge base.'

The suggestion here is that managers tended to regard practitioners' participation in research as an end in itself, and perhaps as a useful avenue for staff development, rather than a potential increment to the agency's capacity to learn lessons. The comments echo those which are often made by external researchers: the 'implementation gap' is evidently not abolished by the researcher's insider position. Interestingly, the need for managers to learn how to make better use of research and to prioritize research activities is conceded by the senior respondents in Sinclair and Jacobs' (1994) study of how research is experienced in local authorities.

While a mixed account emerges about the impact of the research within the agencies, a clearer picture is given of longer-term effects on the practitioners' own approach to their work and to research. Only one respondent declared that after having had a taste of research via the programme, enough was enough, and that he or she had no further interest in research. A number expressed a desire to engage in research full time, and a few had actually done so by leaving practice to embark on a higher degree, a development which, though reflecting well on the programme, in part defeats one of its objects of planting the seeds of research awareness in the world of practice and hoping they will germinate. The rest, when asked about plans for doing further research, were evenly divided between those who said they would like to remain in practice but carry out research from time to time (some of them having already embarked on further work), and those who said they would like a post in which both practice or management and research were explicitly integrated (one or two of them having already obtained such a post).

While some of the reported benefits to people's own work were fairly mundane:

> '[Research] helped me in other parts of my work, e.g. preparation of reports and other practical tips such as using flipcharts to record data and list themes,'

others made some interesting observations about the residue left by participation in research:

> '[Research] has helped to maintain my interest in my practice and continue questioning and developing how we work.'

> 'I enjoy research and think it should be a component of every strand of social work at some stage. It helps towards accountability, gives confidence, and encourages others to notice and value our work.'

> 'The research section continue to be helpful and we approach them regularly for advice, whereas before we may have seen them as rather élite or our own questions as rather trivial.'

> 'I particularly enjoyed the direct link between real practice development and research . . . I find it easier to think in evaluative terms, or to prompt questions that might lead to a research proposal.'

There were also reflections of more tangible effects of practitioners' own increased research awareness:

> 'Other professionals have used me as a consultant to discuss their own small-scale research plans.'

> 'I am quite critical now of questionnaires which are ambiguous or not clear . . . I now fill in questionnaires as fully as possible.'

> 'My current management role involves having an understanding and awareness of the importance of research. It is therefore important to have been through the process of conducting my own research project.'

Such modest gains as these perhaps offer some indication of the kind of longer-term benefits to be looked for if practitioner research is to be developed on a wider front.

Directions and priorities

The benefits noted above – the 'residue' as we put it above of programme participation – are of several kinds. It is apparent that when practitioners undertake research a number of different seeds are sown. Practitioners learn something about their own practice, and if dissemination is effective and audiences receptive (which is not always the case) the extra knowledge is available to their agencies and the wider world of practice. Some of the practitioners emphasize their new-found familiarity with research concepts and techniques, and the ability this gives them to carry out further research, to give advice to others, or to engage on terms approaching equality with those who do. Others claim a capacity to read research more critically, to be more appreciative of what research can and cannot do, and to be more sympathetic than before to approaches from outside for their cooperation in studies. Yet others show awareness of how research is not necessarily remote from their world and might be put to serious use in their practitioner or management roles.

The question has been raised as to what practitioner research primarily constitutes: an extension of practice or an extension of research? This need not, however, be an either/or matter. To some, at least of the tests proposed at the beginning of this chapter, we can give positive responses.

This suggestion has its dangers, but it may be, for much of the indisputably useful increments to the individual and collective resources of practitioners we have identified, that the quality of the research output itself is not of the first importance. There are some constraints in what can be attempted – clearly, it is not easy for basic-grade practitioners to interview the director! Inevitably, we have found that the studies produced by practitioners are variable in achievement, ranging from the carefully and rigorously worked out to more ephemeral and 'softer' pieces. Methodologically, the body of practitioner research produced at Stirling has with some exceptions not been particularly adventurous, in part because our own advice to novice researchers has tended to be that tried, tested and well-understood methods are most likely to be successfully carried through. However, our suspicion that practitioners would be most attracted to the small-scale, perhaps rather cosy, interview-based study, as being what is most familiar to them from their own professional skills, has not been consistently borne out. At the least, practitioners have confounded any sceptical view that practitioner research would prove impossible to bring off at all.

We have sometimes wondered whether our expectations have been too low, in the belief that completing a piece of work somehow is in itself a considerable achievement for beginners working against the odds. At other times, we have wondered whether we have expected too much, especially in terms of the need for practitioners to absorb complex and unfamiliar material in a short space of time. This dilemma will be known to others who have been concerned with practitioner research; participants come with very varied starting points, and the truth is probably somewhere in the middle.

Our instinct, having sown the seeds in the way the book has described, is to let a hundred varied flowers bloom. The potential benefits are multiple, and there is scope for significant expansion of practitioner research, in terms both of small-scale studies to be done which might not attract the attention of professional researchers and of practitioners with an interest in research and the capacity to carry it out, given the appropriate tools. The inhibiting effects of crowded agency agendas and ineluctable pressures on practitioner workloads should not be underestimated, and programmes like ours are probably unlikely to become common. Nevertheless, we are not convinced that scope could not be found for local groups of research-minded practitioners to be fostered, for individual members of agency teams to be designated as having a research promotion or liaison role, for local partnerships between practitioners and academics and/or in-house research staff to be forged – along lines suggested by Whitaker and Archer (1989) – where researchers or their own organizations might need to take initial initiatives. Other ways forward are charted by Connor (1993), with the development of do-it-yourself evaluation kits for practitioners – work primarily aimed at voluntary agencies but containing much that is useful in the statutory sector.

Lest we should be thought to be encouraging an indiscriminate free-for-all, however, it is as well (apart from the seemingly permanent premium on staff time and energy) to sound some more specific warning notes. Most of us can think of areas where professional staff and clients are in such demand as subjects of research scrutiny as to risk being over-researched. Furthermore, a proliferation of research studies which do not meet rudimentary standards of rigour, realism and utility can bring the enterprise into disrepute, doing no good to anyone. There will always be a need, therefore, for some exercise of quality control: to distinguish the promising ideas from the specious, to direct enthusiasm to areas where it is most likely to pay off, to ensure that studies do not proceed without the technical or other support which will be necessary at a later stage. This is a job which may be performed by a formal external advisor of the kind that has been vital to the success of the programme we have described, but there is also a role for in-house researchers in those practice agencies fortunate enough to have such a resource. Research staff in social services and social work departments (sometimes these days going under mystifying titles) are often relatively invisible to main-grade practitioners; but as well as sometimes being able to provide technical support, they have considerable knowledge of departmental research needs, sources of data, and knowledge of previous research that has been undertaken, and in a statutory department are better placed than external researchers to offer sound advice.

Agency research staff are potentially an important bridging mechanism between the worlds of academic research and of policy and practice

– worlds which notoriously do not communicate well with each other, nor fully understand each other's priorities. Despite good intentions and periodic attempts to improve this situation, one suspects that it will always be the case that the relationship will be a problematic one, additionally compounded by the agency and academic politics which sometimes inhibit meetings of senior minds. It is tempting to see the development of a body of practitioner–researchers as a kind of fifth column, moving quietly between the research and the practice domains and in modest ways bringing them closer together.

Finally, we would like to end with a quotation from an unlikely source. In this passage, George Eliot (1855) is talking about intellectual endeavour more generally, but the language she uses makes it seem a remarkably apposite comment on research at large and, perhaps, on practitioner research in particular.

> He is the most effective educator who aims less at perfecting specific requirements than at producing that mental condition which renders acquirements easy and leads to their useful application . . . the most effective writer is not he who demonstrates that this measure is right and that measure wrong, but he who arouses in others the activities that must issue in discovery, who awakes men from their indifference to the right and the wrong, who nerves their energies to seek for the truth and live up to it at whatever cost. The influence of such a writer is dynamic . . . He does not, perhaps, enrich your stock of data, but he clears away the film from your eyes that you may search for data with some purpose. He does not, perhaps, convince you, but he strikes you, undeceives you, animates you.

Practitioners, agencies and topics 1991–95

Fiona Adams and Rona Laing, Fife Social Work Department, *Evaluation of Glenrothes Carers' Support Group*, 1991.

Alana Atkinson, Fife Social Work Department, *To Evaluate the Effectiveness of Divisional Planning Teams in Influencing and Participating in Community Care Planning*, 1994.

Tam Baillie, Strathclyde Social Work Department, *What is the Social Work Agenda for Young People on City Centre Streets?*, 1994.

Gordon Baird and Robert Cook, Central Social Work Department, *A Study of the Process of Assessment of Older People: The CAFE Form as an Assessment Document*, 1991.

Neil Ballantyne, Strathclyde Social Work Department, *Area Team Resource Groups in Strathclyde*, 1991.

Margaret Anne Boyd, Strathclyde Social Work Department, *A Comparison and Evaluation of the History of Children in Care Within Emergency and Temporary Placements*, 1994.

Dorothy Brownlie, Strathclyde Social Work Department, *A Study of Teenage Pregnancy – Trends within Rutherglen Maternity and Issues for Practice*, 1994.

Ruth Burke, Lothian Social Work Department, *How do Social Workers Work with Families of the Children they Receive into Care?*, 1992.

Ian Cairns, Tayside Social Work Department, *An Evaluation of the Referrals to the DART Project from Psychiatric Services*, 1993.

Fiona Campbell, Lothian Family Conciliation Service, *Access Centre Project. A Study of the Users' Perspective*, 1992.

Franki Campbell, Scottish Association for Mental Health, *An Evaluation of the SAMH Family Helper Project from a Client Perspective*, 1992.

Susan Cornish, Millburn West Lothian, *West Lothian Youth Strategy Centre: The First Placements at Millburn*, 1991.

Iain Craig, Fife Social Work Department, *The Evaluation of a Day Centre Resource in Crail*, 1993.

Gail Crawford, Tayside Social Work Department, *Preparing the Way: What Planners and Service Providers Need to Know in Ensuring that 'Practical Support for Carers is a High Priority'*, 1992.

Charlotte Currie, Strathclyde Social Work Department, *Peri-Natal Social Indicators of Babies and Young Children at Risk of Reception into Care*, 1992.

Allan Ferguson and Isobel Hynd, Fife Social Work Department, *A Study of the Effect of a Home Care Project for People with Dementia*, 1992.

Kaye Flockhart, Lothian Social Work Department, *A Comparison of Families' and Therapists' Perceptions of Change Following Family Therapy Being Offered as an Intervention Strategy*, 1991.

Gordon Forsyth, Borders Social Work Department, *Integration? Segregation? How One Local Authority Home For Elderly People in the Borders Works with People Labelled as Suffering from Dementia at the Time of Application for Residential Care*, 1991.

Fiona Garwood, Family Conciliation Scotland, *Study of Rule of Court Referrals to Family Conciliation Services*, 1991.

June Gray, ACET, *Evaluation of Barney's Child Care Work in Dundee*, 1994.

Tony Halpin, Central Region Social Work Department, *An Examination of the Links Between Being 'In Care' and Subsequent Imprisonment*, 1993.

Marie Hayes, Strathclyde Social Work Department, *Residential Rehabilitation – Substance Misuse, What are the Indicators of Person Staying Four Weeks and Over?*, 1993.

Jean Hirst, Lothian Social Work Department, *Routes to Resources: How can they be Improved for Disabled People?*, 1991.

Lesley Houston, Strathclyde SWD (Regional Standby Service), *The Contribution of the Home Care Service to the Regional Standby Service*, 1992.

Patricia Howell, Strathclyde Social Work Department, *Foster Carers: Perceptions and Preferences in Relation to Gender of Children Placed with Them*, 1994.

Anne Irvine, Aberdeen Community Mental Health Team, *The Social Work Role in Relation to Clients with a Diagnosis of Personality Disorder*, 1991.

Amanda James, Central Social Work Department, *A Study of Matching Criteria and Practices in the Community Respite Care Service*, 1991.

Liz Kampman, Independent Needs Assessment and Advocacy Service (Scotland), *An Investigation of the Views of Statutory Agencies, the Voluntary Sector and Users of Services on the Value of an Independent Needs Assessment and Professional Representation Service*, 1994.

Sheila Kerr, Church of Scotland, *Invereck Residential Home*, 1994.

Marjut Kosonen, Tayside Social Work Department, *Evaluation of Foster and Adoptive Care Services in Tayside*, 1992.

Gordon Lockerbie, Grampian Social Work Department, *Does a Programme of Groupwork Based on Relevant Theory in a Respite and Day Care Setting Improve Specific Behaviours of People with Dementia?*, 1993.

Maureen Lynch, Family Mediation Scotland, *The Role of Local Family Mediation and Conciliation Services in Meeting the Needs of Children whose Parents Separate or Divorce*, 1993.

Sue MacFadyen, Barnardo's New Families Project, *Preparing or Deterring?: Consumer Feedback on Preparation Groups for Prospective Adoptive Parents*, 1991.

Cameron MacVicar, Aberlour Child Care Trust, *Increasing Choice? Evaluation of a Part-Time Residential Respite Care Service for Children/Young People with Learning Difficulties Based in Dunfermline*, 1991.

John McBride, Lothian Social Work Department, *Perceptions of Social Workers Using Psychiatric Teams*, 1994.

Peter McCann, Strathclyde Social Work Department, *Community Service – An Alternative to Custody?*, 1994.

Delores McFadden, Fife Social Work Department, *Role of OT with CVA Client Treatment and Enhancing Quality of Life*, 1994.

May McGhee, Strathclyde SWD (Glasgow Royal Infirmary), *Evaluation of a Hospital Based Counselling Services for Infertile People*, 1992.

Dee Miller, Grampian SWD (Aberdeen Community Mental Health Team), *Evaluation of Treatment/Intervention for those Suffering from Eating Disorders*, 1992.

Sue Mills, Family Care (Family Link Project), *Family Link Scheme*, 1992.

Sue Milne, Edinburgh Family Service Unit, *Children's Levels of Participation in a 'Children's Rights' Group*, 1994.

Fraser Mitchell, Strathclyde Social Work Department, *Carers' Groups: A Comparative Study*, 1993.

Sandra Moody, National Foster Care Association, *An Evaluation of the Effectiveness of NFCA's Counselling and Conciliation Project in Meeting the Needs of Carers in Difficulty*, 1993.

Gillian Moreton, Central Region Social Work Department, *Social Work Practice and Policy on Access and Reunion between Children and Relatives who have been Convicted of Sexual Offences*, 1993.

Joan Murray, Grampian Social Work Department, *Evaluation of Community Service Orders*, 1993.

Linda Paterson, Family Care, *A Survey of Adoptive Parents and Adopted People's Attitudes Towards Birth Parents*, 1992.

Cathy Phillips-Conoby, The SACRO/UVAF Volunteer Project, Central Region, *Prison Befriending: The Impact of Volunteer Befrienders Working with Prisoners*, 1992.

Jill Pritchard, Fife Social Work Department, *To Assess the Effectiveness of OT Response to Bathing Assessment Requests*, 1993.

Rod Richard, Highland Social Work Department, *Relative Stress Experienced by Social Workers in Different Settings*, 1993.

Hazel Robertson, Tayside Social Work Department, *Respite Care – Assessing the Need in Tayside*, 1993.

Rona Robertson, RSPCC, *The Ettrick Study*, 1991.

Sarah Sieley, Lothian Social Work Department, *Evaluating Effectiveness of Coordinated Assessment*, 1992.

Joanne Sinclair, SACRO, *An Evaluative Study of SACRO's Alcohol Project for Probationers*, 1992.

Jean Smith, Royal Hospital for Sick Children, *Listening to Families of Children with Cancer: Perceptions of Social Work Help*, 1991.

Mark Smith, Lothian Social Work Department, *Evaluation of the First Year of Pentland View Close Support Unit*, 1993.

Fiona Southern, Malcolm Sargent Social Work Team, *To Investigate the Effects of Treatment for a Brain Tumour on Children and their Families*, 1994.

Brian Stevenson, Fife Social Work Department, *Child Protection Case Conferences. Parents' Perspective – The Fife Experience*, 1992.

Fiona Stewart, Tayside Social Work Department, *Needs of People with Hearing Impairment in Local Authority Residential Homes for Older People*, 1993.

Stephanie Stone, Strathclyde Social Work Department, *Explaining Adoption – What are the Difficulties Experienced by Adoptive Parents?*, 1994.

Beryl Thomson, Fife Social Work Department, *Carers' Perceptions of Occupational Therapy Services to the Terminally Ill Following Bereavement*, 1994.

Andy Wales, Strathclyde Social Work Department, *A Qualitative Study of the Motoring Project from the Viewpoint and Experiences of the Client Group*, 1994.

Irene Werritty, Aberlour Child Care Trust, *Day Care – The Relationship Between Caregiver and Parent*, 1993.

Neill Williamson and Marlene Milne, Grampian Social Work Department, *'Boiling Point'*, 1993.

Jim Wilson, Lothian Social Work Department, *Consumer and Practitioner Feedback on a Social Work Office Duty System*, 1991.

Catherine Young, Dumfries and Galloway Social Work Department, *Extended Opening of Annan Day Care Centre*, 1993.

Appendix 2

Practitioner research programme: Annotated bibliography

Addison, C. (1988) *Planning Investigative Projects: A Workbook for Social Services Practitioners*. London: NISW.
A down-to-earth, practical and relatively brief guide, covering the development of a proposal (with useful worksheets) and some remarks on methods, with a stress on the qualitative. Note: This will be supplied to programme participants; it contains an annotated bibliography, to which this is a supplement.

Cheetham, J., Fuller, R., McIvor, G. and Petch, A. (1993) *Evaluating Social Work Effectiveness*. Buckingham: Open University Press.
Purports to be the definitive current text on researching social work – a comprehensive review of evaluative approaches, methods, problems and potential.

Connor, A. (1993) *Monitoring and Evaluation Made Easy*. London: HMSO.
A simple and practical guide in plain language, subtitled 'a handbook for voluntary organisations' and focusing on small projects, with numerous examples of evaluative ideas and instruments.

Edwards, A. and Talbot, R. (1994) *The Hard-Pressed Researcher*. London: Longman.
Described as 'a research handbook for the caring professions', this book contains useful advice about the general approach to research. Parts of it will probably be more technical than most people will find useful.

Fisher, M. (ed.) (1983) *Speaking of Clients*. JUSSR University of Sheffield/Community Care.
A useful collection of papers about studying the user perspective, which is both reflective and practice-oriented. Includes contributions by Eric Sainsbury (the doyen of client studies – see below), Tim Booth and Mike Fisher.

Goldberg, E.M. and Connolly, N. (1981) *Evaluative Research in Social Care*. London: Heinemann Educational Books.
Another collection of academic papers which report research and illustrate different methodological approaches, and one of the basic texts on evaluative research.

Herbert, M. (1990) *Planning a Research Project: A Guide for Practitioners and Trainees in The Helping Profession.* London: Cassell.
With origins in clinical psychology, this volume is weighted towards more quantitative approaches. It is particularly good for a quick entry to statistical analysis.

Kane, E. (1985) *Doing Your Own Research.* London: Marion Boyars.
Another basic and user-friendly guide to the inexperienced researcher.

Lishman, J. (ed.) (1984) *Research Highlights 8: Evaluation,* 2nd edn. London: Jessica Kingsley.
A collection of academic papers on different aspects of the theory and practice of evaluation aiming to represent different designs and methods (e.g. controlled experiments, illuminative evaluation, cost-effectiveness, etc.). Contains the important and influential paper by Smith and Cantley on pluralistic evaluation.

McDowell, I. and Newall, C. (1987) *Measuring Health: A Guide to Rating Scales and Questionnaires.* Oxford: Oxford University Press.
Health in this volume is treated broadly with the scales reviewed dealing with functional disability, psychological well-being, social health (via social support and social adjustment) and quality of life as well as physical illness. Conceptual and practical issues are clearly discussed but the book is more suitable for those with some research experience than for complete novices.

Milne, D. (ed.) (1987) *Evaluating Mental Health Practice Methods and Applications.* London: Croom Helm.
Aimed at mental health practitioners, a general introduction on principles of evaluation is followed by chapters contributed from a range of disciplines (including social workers) which provide an interesting overview and comparison of different strategies.

Patton, M.Q. (1980) *Qualitative Evaluation Methods.* London: Sage.
An American book with features that some will find irritating, others attractive! A plea for qualitative evaluation methods, which many assume (wrongly, according to the author) do not carry conviction with policymakers; contains many examples, though few are drawn from social services.

Phillips, C., Palfrey, C. and Thomas, P. (1994) *Evaluating Health and Social Care.* London: Macmillan.
A straightforward text for those looking for a basic introduction to the principles and practice of evaluation. Liberal use of examples.

Robson, C. (1993) *Real World Research.* Oxford: Blackwell.
A lengthy, comprehensive and useful guide, well illustrated by examples, to a wide range of research methods and approaches. Although pitched at a more advanced level than that of many practitioner–researchers, this book is recommended for those who wish to dig deeper into research methodology.

Sainsbury, E. (1987) Client studies: their contribution and limitations in influencing social work practice, *British Journal of Social Work,* 17: 635–44.
Sainsbury reflects on the methodological lessons to be learnt from client studies, seeks to clarify how they can be used, and suggests ways forward.

Sheldon, B. (1986) Social work effectiveness experiments: review and implications, *British Journal of Social Work*, 16: 223–42.
A well-known review of evaluative research on social work which challenges the widely held view that social work emerges badly from studies of its effectiveness. Sheldon argues that when social work activities are clearly focused, problems clearly identified and modest and specified goals set with clients, then carefully controlled studies produce positive results.

Streiner, D.L. and Norman, G.R. (1989) *Health Measurement Scales: A Practical Guide to their Development and Use.* Oxford: Oxford University Press.
This is a useful critical review of a number of scales which can be used in social work research with some straightforward discussion of issues to consider in their selection. The hazards and possibilities of developing new scales are also explored thoroughly and practically.

Whittaker, D.S. and Archer, J.L. (1989) *Research by Social Workers: Capitalising on Experience.* London: CCETSW.
Covers the same ground as Addison (ibid.), but in much more detail – sometimes excessive in view of its target audience – and contains much that is useful. The book is very generous in the use of everyday examples, and covers a wide range of methods of data collection and analysis. Again, useful worksheets.

Appendix 3

Brief glossary

Action research   A partnership between researchers and practitioners in a jointly planned series of stages incorporating a feedback loop in which the results of research inform the development of practice.

Case   An individual member of a research sample (q.v.).

Coding   The process by which raw data (q.v.), i.e. data in the form in which it is originally collected, is ordered into a form in which it can be analysed: usually a question of assigning individual responses into more general or standardized categories.

Control group   A group of research subjects in an experimental research design. The 'experimental' group received a particular treatment or intervention, and the outcomes are compared with those of a control group, composed of similar cases, who have received no such treatment or intervention. Equivalence between the groups being achieved through random allocation (hence 'RCT' or randomized controlled experiment).

Comparison group   A looser term than control group (q.v.), but a device often more feasible to use, a comparison group is a second group receiving either no intervention or different intervention studied alongside the sample of main interest in order to draw comparisons. Random allocation is not involved.

Data   Items of information assembled by researchers through the medium of questionnaires, interviews, or other instruments. Data may be collected in a relatively structured form, in which case it is already located in categories determined by the researcher, or in a relatively unstructured form, often in words chosen by respondents, as in the case of narrative or the replies to open-ended questions.

Effectiveness   The extent to which an activity achieves its objectives (q.v.); often bracketed with efficiency and equity (q.v.) as 'the three Es'.

Efficiency   The maximization of ends from given means.

Equity   The fair distribution of resources.

Evaluation   Assessing the value of an activity: evaluating an activity is thus a more ambitious undertaking than studying its effectiveness (q.v.).

Hypothesis   A proposition about the social world or about intervention, often in the form 'X is the result of Y', that the researcher wishes to test by collecting data that would confirm or (more probably) refute it.

Instrument A device for collecting data: interview schedules, questionnaires, case review forms or other pro formas, observation schedules, diaries, etc.

Objective The stated goal of an activity.

Outcome The demonstrable effect or consequence of an activity; strictly speaking, therefore, outcomes need not only to be measured but to be causally related to the activity in question.

Participative research A style of research in which the subjects of study actively contribute to the selection of research questions and the choice of design and methods.

Pilot A trial run of a research instrument (q.v.) which enables the researcher to detect any flaws in the questionnaire, interview schedule or other data-collection device. An essential stage in the design of instruments.

Pluralistic evaluation An approach to evaluation which assesses the value of an activity as variously defined by the different parties having a stake in the activity; differences in perspective between stakeholders are assumed to be the norm rather than the exception.

Qualitative Refers to data or analysis which is rich in the detail or particularity of individuals' experiences, perceptions or definitions of their situation, often with a small sample. Qualitative data may, however, be analysed quantitatively by means of careful coding.

Quantitative Refers to data which is in numerical form, lending itself to producing frequency counts, averages and percentages, and which may be analysed by statistical methods.

Reliability A measure of consistency in data collection and analysis. A question, scale, or instrument is reliable if repeated administration of it would produce the same results. Assigning data to categories is reliable if different analysts reach the same decisions ('inter-rater reliability').

Sample A group selected from a wider population in such a way as to be representative of it or of specified parts of it; sampling is a device to enable statements to be made about a population without the need to collect data on all members of the population.

Statistical significance A mathematical calculation which establishes whether a particular distribution of cases between variables has occurred by chance, often used to clarify whether potentially causal associations between variables occur. There is a range of tests of significance appropriate for different kinds of data.

Theory A set of connected ideas or propositions held to explain observed phenomena. Research is often criticized for not being sufficiently theoretically informed, by which is usually meant an absence of a theoretical base generating hypotheses (q.v.) or research questions which are then subjected to testing by the research in order to throw further light on the theory being investigated.

Triangulation A term often used loosely to mean variously: using more than one question to investigate a variable, using more than one method for collecting data on the same set of variables, or using more than one source of data.

Validity Broadly, the capacity of an instrument to measure what it purports to measure, or what the researcher believes it to measure.

Variable A term researchers give to key factors or concepts that they wish to investigate. Strictly speaking variables are abstract and cannot be measured directly. Before data can be collected variables need to be 'operationalized' by identifying indicators which stand for them. Indicators for the variable 'social inclusion' might include types and frequency of visitors, participation in activities outside the home, membership of groups, and so on. An 'independent variable' is one hypothesized to cause the incidence of a 'dependent variable', though the analysis may be complicated by intermediate or 'intervening variables'.

Bibliography

Addison, C. (1988) *Planning Investigative Projects: A Workbook for Social Services Practitioners*. London: NISW.

Becker, H.S. (1986) *Writing for Social Scientists*. Chicago and London: University of Chicago Press.

Bell, C. and Encel, S. (eds) (1978) *Inside the Whale: Ten Personal Accounts of Social Research*. Oxford: Pergamon Press.

Bell, C. and Newby, H. (eds) (1977) *Doing Sociological Research*. London: Allen and Unwin.

Bell, C. and Roberts, H. (eds) (1984) *Social Researching, Politics, Problems, Practice*. London: Routledge and Kegan Paul.

Black, J. (1992) *User Involvement in Mental Health Services: An Annotated Bibliography 1985–1992*. Birmingham: University of Birmingham.

Black, J., Bowl, R., Critcher, C., Grant, G. and Stockford, D. (1983) *Social Work in Context*. London: Tavistock.

Black, T.R. (1993) *Evaluating Social Science Research*. London: Sage.

Bowling, A. (1991) *Measuring Health*. Buckingham: Open University Press.

Broad, B. and Fletcher, C. (eds) (1993) *Practitioner Social Work Research in Action*. London: Whiting and Birch.

Brown, S. and McIntyre, D. (1993) *Making Sense of Teaching*. Buckingham: Open University Press.

Bryman, A. and Cramer, D. (1994) *Quantitative Data Analysis for Social Scientists* (rev. edn). London: Routledge.

Burgess, R.G. (1984) *In the Field: An Introduction to Field Research*. London: Allen and Unwin.

Central Council for Education and Training of Social Workers (1989) *Requirements and Regulations for the Diploma in Social Work: Paper No. 30*. London: CCETSW.

Challis, D. and Chesterman, J. (1985) A system for monitoring social work activity with the frail elderly, *British Journal of Social Work*, 15: 115–32.

Cheetham, J., Fuller, R., McIvor, G. and Petch, A. (1992) *Evaluating Social Work Effectiveness*. Buckingham: Open University Press.

Connor, A. (1993) *Monitoring and Evaluation Made Easy. A Handbook for Voluntary Organisations*. Edinburgh: HMSO.

Department of Health (1994) *A Wider Strategy for Research and Development Relating to Personal Social Services*. London: HMSO.

Dey, I. (1993) *Qualitative Data Analysis*. London: Routledge.

Edwards, A. and Talbot, R. (1994) *The Hard-Pressed Researcher*. London: Longman.

Eliot, G. (1855) Thomas Carlyle, in Pinney, T. (ed.) (1963) *Essays of George Eliot*. London: Routledge and Kegan Paul.

Elliott, J. (1991) *Action Research for Educational Change*. Milton Keynes: Open University Press.

Everitt, A., Hardiker, P., Littlewood, J. and Mullender, A. (1992) *Applied Research for Better Practice*. London: Macmillan.

Ford, J. (1975) *Paradigms and Fairy Tales: An Introduction to the Science of Meanings*, Vols 1 and 2. London: Routledge and Kegan Paul.

Fuller, R. and Tulle-Winton, E. (forthcoming) Genericism, specialism and others, *British Journal of Social Work*.

Goldberg, E.M. and Connolly, N. (eds) (1981) *Evaluative Research in Social Care*. London: Heinemann.

Goldberg, E.M. and Warburton, R.W. (1979) *Ends and Means in Social Work*. London: George Allen and Unwin.

Gutek, B. (1978) Strategies for studying client satisfaction, *Journal of Social Issues*, 34: 44–56.

Harding, T. and Upton, A. (1991) *User Involvement in Social Services: An Annotated Bibliography*. London: NISW.

Herbert, M. (1990) *Planning a Research Project – A Guide for Practitioners and Trainees in the Helping Professions*. London: Cassell.

Howie, J.G.R. (1989) *Research in General Practice*. London: Chapman and Hall.

Hunt, S. (1992) A British adaptation of the General Well-being Index: a new tool for clinical research, *British Journal of Medical Economics*, 2: 49–60.

Kemmis, S. and McTaggart, T. (1981) *The Action Research Planner*. Geelong: Deakin University Press.

Knapp, M. (1984) *The Economics of Social Care*. London: Macmillan.

Lawton, M. P. (1975) Philadelphia Geriatric Center Morale Scale: A revision, *Journal of Gerontology*, 30: 85–9.

Lehman, A.F. (1983) The well-being of chronic mental patients: assessing their quality of life, *Archives of General Psychiatry*, 40: 369–73.

Lishman, J. (ed.) (1984) *Research Highlights: Evaluation*. London: Jessica Kingsley.

Lofland, J. and Lofland, L. (1984) *Analyzing Social Settings: A Guide to Qualitative Observation and Analysis*. Belmont, California: Wadsworth.

Macdonald, G. and Sheldon, B. (1992) Contemporary studies of the effectiveness of social work, *British Journal of Social Work*, 22: 615–44.

McDowell, I. and Newell, C. (1987) *Measuring Health: A Guide to Rating Scales and Questionnaires*. Oxford: Oxford University Press.

McKeganey, N.P. and Bloor, M.J. (1981) On the retrieval of sociological description: respondent validation and the critical case of ethnomethodology, *International Journal of Sociology and Social Policy*, 1: 58–69.

MacPherson, I.A. and Williamson, P.J. (1992) Not quite what I meant – techniques of respondent validation, *Research Policy and Planning*, 10: 10–13.

Petch, A. (1988) Answering back: parental perspectives on the children's hearings system, *British Journal of Social Work*, 18: 1–24.

Phillips, C., Palfrey, C. and Thomas, P. (1994) *Evaluating Health and Social Care.* London: Macmillan.

Rapoport, R.N. (1970) Three dilemmas in action research, *Human Relations,* 23: 499–513.

Richardson, A., Jackson, C. and Sykes, W. (1990) *Taking Research Seriously.* London: HMSO.

Robson, C. (1993) *Real World Research.* Oxford: Blackwell.

Sainsbury, E. (1987) Client studies: their contribution and limitations in influencing social work practice, *British Journal of Social Work,* 17: 635–44.

Schon, D. (1983) *The Reflective Practitioner: How Professionals Think in Action.* London: Temple Smith.

Shakespeare, P., Atkinson, D. and French, S. (eds) (1993) *Reflecting on Research Practice: Issues in Health and Social Welfare.* Buckingham: Open University Press.

Sinclair, R. and Jacobs, C. (1994) *Research in Personal Social Services.* London: National Children's Bureau.

Smith, G. and Cantley, C. (1984) Pluralistic evaluation, in Lishman, J. (ed.) *Research Highlights 8: Evaluation.* London: Jessica Kingsley.

Smith, G. and Cantley, C. (1985) *Assessing Health Care.* Buckingham: Open University Press.

Social Work Research Centre (1993) *Practitioner Research Programme 1991–92: Summary Reports.* Stirling: University of Stirling.

Social Work Research Centre (1994) *Practitioner Research Programme 1993–94: Summary Reports.* Stirling: University of Stirling.

Tesch, R. (1990) *Qualitative Research: Analysis Types and Software Tools.* Basingstoke: Falmer Press.

Twigg, J. and Atkin, K. (1994) *Carers Perceived.* Buckingham: Open University Press.

Warr, P. (1990) The measurement of well-being and other aspects of mental health, *Journal of Occupational Psychology,* 63: 193–210.

Watt, G. (1993) The Chief Scientist reports – making research make a difference, *Health Bulletin,* 51: 187–94.

Whitaker, D.S. and Archer, J.L. (1989) *Research by Social Workers: Capitalizing on Experience.* London: CCETSW.

Index

DOING YOUR RESEARCH PROJECT (2nd edition)
A GUIDE FOR FIRST-TIME RESEARCHERS IN
EDUCATION AND SOCIAL SCIENCE

Judith Bell

If you are a beginner researcher, the problems facing your are much the same whether you are producing a small project, an MEd dissertation or a PhD thesis. You will need to select a topic; identify the objectives of your study; plan and design a suitable methodology; devise research instruments; negotiate access to institutions, material and people; collect, analyse and present information; and finally, produce a well-written report or dissertation. Whatever the scale of the undertaking, you will have to master techniques and devise a plan of action which does not attempt more than the limitations of expertise, time and access permit.

We all learn to do research by actually doing it, but a great deal of time can be wasted and goodwill dissipated by inadequate preparation. This book aims to provide you with the tools to do the job, to help you avoid some of the pitfalls and time-wasting false trails that can eat into your time, to establish good research habits, and to take you from the stage of choosing a topic through to the production of a well-planned, methodologically sound and well-written final report or dissertation on time.

Doing Your Research Project serves as a source of reference and guide to good practice for all beginner researchers, whether undergraduate and postgraduate students or professionals such as teachers or social workers undertaking investigations in Education and the Social Sciences. This second edition retains the basic structure of the very successful first edition whilst incorporating some important new material.

Contents
Introduction – Approaches to educational research – Planning the project – Keeping records and making notes – Reviewing the literature – Negotiating access and the problems of inside research – The analysis of documentary evidence – Designing and administering questionnaires – Planning and conducting interviews – Diaries – Observation studies – Interpretation and presentation of the evidence – Postscript – References – Index.

192pp   0 335 19094 4 (Paperback)

ACTION RESEARCH FOR HEALTH AND SOCIAL CARE
A GUIDE TO PRACTICE

Elizabeth Hart and Meg Bond

- What is action research and how can it best be understood?
- How can practitioners use action research to deal with problems and improve services?
- What are the different types of action research and which might be most appropriate for use in a particular setting?

This book has been designed for use as a core text on research methods courses at undergraduate and postgraduate level and on professional training courses. It is divided into three parts. Part one traces the history of action research and shows the links between its use in education, community development, management research and nursing. Building on this background the book explores different ways in which action research has been defined and proposes four different types, each appropriate to a different problem situation and context. In part two, five case studies of action research are described from the perspective of the researcher, including case studies of success and instructive failure. Part three is designed to enable the reader to find a route through the maze of methods and approaches in action research by the use of such things as self-assessment and mapping exercises, a guide to diary keeping and to evaluation. The final chapter suggests that by developing a 'project perspective' action research can be of practical benefit to health and social care professionals in promoting service improvements.

Contents
Part I: Action research in context, process and practice – Introduction and overview – Action research in context – Action research in process – Action research in practice – Part II: Action research case studies – Case study 1: Micro-politics of action research at a district general hospital – Case study 2: From sister to manager – empowerment through a staff development programme – Case study 3: 'Sitting in the circle' – working across professional boundaries and with older people in the community – Case study 4: Progress and procrastination – using a project group to implement changes in service provision for people with disabilities – Case study 5: Changing medication practices in a home for older people – Part III: Working from a project perspective – Toolkit – Conclusion – Bibliography – Index.

256pp   0 335 19262 9 (Paperback)   0 335 19263 7 (Hardback)

RESEARCH METHODS FOR NURSES AND THE CARING PROFESSIONS
Roger Sapsford and Pamela Abbott

This book is about the appreciation, evaluation and conduct of social research. Aimed at nurses, social workers, community workers and others in the caring professions, the book concentrates on relatively small-scale studies which can be carried out by one or two people, rather than large and well-resourced teams. The authors have provided many short, practical exercises within the text and particular emphasis is given to evaluative research including the assessment of the reader's own professional practice. Their clear, accessible style will make this the ideal introductory text for those undertaking research or the evaluation of research for the first time.

This book may be read in conjunction with *Research into Practice: A Reader for Nurses and the Caring Professions* (Open University Press) by the same authors.

Contents
Section 1: Introduction – Finding out and making sense – Section 2: Assessing research – Reading research reports – Reading open interviewing research – Reading observation research – Reading about controlled trials – Reading survey research – Reading secondary-source research – Section 3: Doing research – Using secondary sources – Survey research: design and sampling – Experimental practice – Open interviewing – Analysing text – Participant observation and self-evaluation – Evaluation of single cases – Section 4: In conclusion – Writing up – In conclusion – References – Index.

192pp   0 335 09620 4 (Paperback)   0 335 09621 2 (Hardback)